Getting into
Character

Getting into Character

The *Art* of First-Person Narrative Preaching

Stephen Chapin Garner

BrazosPress

Grand Rapids, Michigan

© 2008 Stephen Chapin Garner

Published by Brazos Press
a division of Baker Publishing Group
P.O. Box 6287, Grand Rapids, MI 49516-6287
www.brazospress.com

Printed in the United States of America

Library of Congress Cataloging-in-Publication Data
Garner, Stephen Chapin, 1969–
     Getting into character : the art of first-person narrative preaching /
Stephen Chapin Garner.
        p.   cm.
     Includes bibliographical references (p   ).
     ISBN 978-1-58743-218-7 (pbk.)
     1. Narrative preaching. 2. First person narrative. I. Title.
BV4235.S76G37 2008
251—dc22   2007046995

For Tammie,
who has been the spiritual editor
of every sermon I have ever preached

Contents

9

Foreword

Preachers and actors share several things in common. Both communicate ideas. Both stand on a platform, and both speak before an audience. There are also differences. William Charles Macready, the noted English actor of the nineteenth century, wondered why ministers often preached truth as though it were fiction while actors presented fiction as though it were truth. Insofar as that question reflects an accurate observation, it should make thoughtful preachers stop and ponder.

Expositors of the scripture may dismiss the question out of hand. After all, look at the material we are given to work with. Actors have a great advantage. They work with drama that reflects the stuff of life, but preachers must work with more abstract theological concepts that are much less interesting.

That seems like a shallow response to Macready's observation! After all, in the scriptures God communicated himself to us through drama written by theologians who were ripping good storytellers. They chose their material with a great degree of freedom. The Holy Book they wrote is filled with stories about unholy characters whom we would never allow to serve on the official board of our church. We would expect to bump into many of them at a police station. Most are products of dysfunctional families, so it should not surprise us that they are guilty of drunkenness, seduction, rape, and murder. A few are defined by one craven act of cowardice, but others overcome their backgrounds to act with courage against overwhelming odds. God has filled his stage with these shadowy characters that he sometimes describes as men and women of faith. Some theologians would be happier if the Bible were written with outlines indented with points and subpoints. They regard these Old and New Testament stories as theology poorly written.

Let's face it. The difference between the preacher and the playwright isn't primarily the content he or she has to work with, but how that content is presented. All of us have more to learn from people in the theater than we realize. Chapin Garner is a preacher and a pastor, but he has also written and acted in plays. He has written this fascinating book to improve our skill at preparing and presenting first-person narrative sermons. But he does more. He provides workable leads on how you and I can preach the Bible as though it is indeed God's revelation wrapped up in the business of life.

Haddon W. Robinson

Preface

Pitching a Sermon

Martin Copenhaver, a friend and mentor, and a truly fine preacher, once told me that his weekly goal for the sermon moment was simply to "get on base." He wanted to get a "base hit." Being a young and naïve preacher at the time, I was taken aback by the thought that a preacher wouldn't swing for the fences every time he or she entered the pulpit. Why set such a modest goal? However, as every baseball fan can tell you, those batters with the chronic home-run swing strike out often, and those hitters who have high on-base percentages are invaluable and highly productive members of the team. Martin Copenhaver's preaching philosophy has allowed him to be one of the most consistent preachers I have ever encountered. During the years in which I had the opportunity to listen to Martin's sermons, I always left Sunday worship feeling as though the Holy Spirit had said something to me through the sermon moment. Martin consistently gets on base, and he hits his fair share of home runs, too.

For years, when sharing sermons with colleagues, we would employ this baseball lingo in the critique of our messages. A sermon would start out clearly, the introduction would be captivating, good mileage could be made of the homiletical idea, but the message fell short of expectations, and we'd say: "You got good wood on the ball—but you lined out to shallow left." Of a sermon with a modest amount of artistry and illustration that still made a solid point or impact, we'd say, "You're on base." If a sermon made a clear point, had solid application to daily life, and was tied up with a memorable story or illustration, we'd say, "You've got a stand-up double." We have found we have many responses to different sermons: "It's a fielder's choice." "You fouled that one off." "Ground rule double." "You're sliding into third." "You're swinging at air." Sometimes the scripture combined with a powerful homiletical idea and an important community or life event allows for that rare and extraordinary sermon of which we say, "It's outta here—it's going to land in another zip code!" This, of course, is a way of expressing our subjective opinion on sermon quality; it does not address the style of delivery, which is actually the most important part of any baseball game.

Pitching, and having a pitcher who has command of different types of delivery, is easily the most essential component of any baseball team. Even a great fastball pitcher won't last long in the big leagues unless he has a solid breaking ball and perhaps an effective change-up. I have realized that the preaching art is much more akin to pitching than it is to hitting. We take the biblical text, and through prayer, exegesis, and thoughtful reflection we come up with a homiletical idea that serves as the strike zone for our sermon. The next question we need to ask ourselves is, Which homiletical style of delivery will best serve my congregation on a given Sunday? Will a deductive, an inductive, a narrative, or a first-person sermon style best communicate the homiletical idea? I have come to believe that, like an effective pitcher, a preacher's ability to command several different styles of delivery helps to make the sermon moment more dynamic and memorable. I have come to understand the deductive sermon as my personal "fastball"—I tell the congregation where we are going, and then work to bring that message directly to them without deviation. An inductive sermon is a "curve ball"—a message initially seems to bend in a different direction only to wind up falling into the strike zone. For me, the "change-up" has come in the form of first-person narrative sermons, and it is this style of delivery that I will focus on in this volume. This is a sermon form that can often take people by surprise. They assume a traditional form, only to find the sermon delivered in the voice and person of Peter, or Elijah, or Ruth, or a present-day or fictional person. A first-person narrative sermon is a message that communicates a scriptural or homiletical idea through a character other than one's self. It is a style of storytelling where the preacher takes on the personality and voice of another—preferably, I will argue, the personality of a *biblical* character. I want to encourage you to include first-person narrative sermons in your preaching/pitching repertoire. I also want to prepare you and give you resources, so that you are able to thoroughly enjoy and pursue excellence in first-person narrative preaching.

Our people desire and deserve effective preaching of the gospel of Jesus Christ. It is often helpful to lead them through a scriptural or homiletical idea by a variety of different approaches. If a congregation is so used to the pattern and style of a pastor's preaching that they know how the sermon is going to end before the sermon begins, the strike zone is missed, and the congregation is in danger of being mindlessly walked. We don't want our

15

people to walk out the sanctuary doors without striking at their heart with the Word of God. First-person narrative preaching can be a powerful sermonic pitch that allows the Word of God to unexpectedly strike and stick in the hearts and minds of our people.

1

The Power and Problem of First-Person Biblical Narrative in Preaching

The Power of Biblical Story

Every Christian leader and preacher has a story of how they came to faith. There was a particular church, or a particular pastor, or a particular moment through which we clergy sensed the spirit of God moving in our lives, and through that movement our awareness of God and our desire to follow Christ was born. For me, the experience came by way of a gift. When I was six or seven years old, my parents gave me my first record player, and my mother gave me her well-worn set of Bible-story records. They were a set of eight records that fit nicely into a cardboard box that was adorned with a colorful image of Jesus teaching by the Sea of Galilee. On those records were etched the stories of David and Goliath; Daniel in the lion's den; Noah and the ark; Jonah and the whale; Shadrach, Meshach, and Abednego and the fiery furnace; and several other foundational Bible stories. After school, I would run up to my room, close my door, and place one of these records on my player. The record would pop and crackle, and then the story would begin. I sat with rapt attention as David released the stone from his sling, and the stone landed with a *thwap* on Goliath's forehead. I loved the sound of the thundering rain as God told Noah to nail the door of the ark shut. The roaring flames of the fiery furnace made me cringe, but I perked up when I heard the voices of Shadrach, Meshach, and Abednego praising God without a hair on their heads being singed. The dramatic telling of the biblical story captivated me, and through those stories—through those characters—I encountered the presence and power of the living God.

The power of story to ignite our God-given imaginations is remarkable. We are drawn in by well-crafted characters. We sit on the edge of our seats when plots thicken and twist. We are a people who long for and devour stories. Stories printed in the pages of a book, dramas brought to life on the stage, plotlines drawn on television and cinema screens—all these hold great sway in our lives. Story, character, and plot are powerful vehicles of communication. Many churches and pastors have realized the importance and effectiveness of communicating messages through different forms of media. Sermons that utilize film clips, worship that incorporates fast-paced video storytelling, and adult education classes that use PowerPoint presentations to convey the gospel message are commonplace in our country. Why simply *tell* people about the story, when you can *show* them the story?

Showing the Story

I want to encourage you to consider employing a type of preaching that literally *shows* people the gospel story. In fact, I want you to consider using a style of preaching that will not only introduce your people to the gospel story, but also introduce your congregation to biblical characters. First-person narrative preaching is a style of sermon delivery that not only brings the Word of God to life; but brings the characters of the Bible to life in ways that can illustrate gospel messages with extraordinary and memorable power. When done well, with great care given to both artistry and faithful exegesis, you can allow biblical characters to leap from the pages of your Bible and into the aisles of your sanctuary. In first-person narrative preaching, the preacher takes on the personality and voice of a biblical character to share a homiletical message with a congregation. From the pulpit, from the chancel, or from the aisles, characters such as Ruth, David, Moses, Sarah, Elizabeth, Peter, and Paul have the ability to connect with, and impart a message to, actively engaged church members. The pastors who have mastered the art of first-person narrative preaching know that these sermons are often the most memorable sermons they give. Years after these messages have been shared, congregants will still reminisce about the time Elijah showed up in their sanctuary. And best of all, often they still remember the idea the preacher was trying to communicate! Furthermore, through first-person narrative preaching, you can literally show people the biblical stories and characters without the expense and complexity of film, video, and PowerPoint production. Anyone who is committed to sound exegetical sermon preparation, and who is willing to spend some time examining the keys to effective development of dramatic monologue, can preach powerfully effective first-person narrative sermons.

19

Resistance to First-Person Preaching

It may be that you are very familiar with this kind of sermon style; in fact, you may have seen preachers attempt first-person narrative sermons with regrettable results. I will never forget the first time I preached a first-person narrative sermon. It was very well received, and people greeted me after worship sharing how the sermon had drawn them into the biblical story with a clarity they had not experienced before. Then Judith approached me. Judith came through the receiving line, gave me a big hug, and said, "Chapin, that was a nice sermon. It reminded me of a pastor I used to know. He loved to play different characters during worship—he did it all the time. The congregation didn't appreciate it all that much, but he loved it!" Ouch. I am well aware that there are some pastors who fancy themselves thespians— they are frustrated actors who once had a lead in the high school play and now force their congregation to be their audience. When a sermon is delivered to satisfy a pastor's need instead of working to address the needs of God's people—no matter what the style of delivery—the sermon moment is defiled, and the pastor fails his or her high and holy calling.

I also know that some pastors are reluctant to attempt a first-person narrative sermon because they fear looking foolish. The last thing they want to do is dress up like the poorly costumed children in last year's Christmas pageant. Costumes and props, are, of course, optional—in fact, I will argue against their use altogether in chapter 6. This reluctance, however, is often an easy excuse for a deeper discomfort. Pastors get in comfortable and well-worn patterns of sermon preparation and delivery. The mere idea of breaking the routine and taking a risk on a new sermon style only increases the already anxious process of readying the weekly message.

I have seen, heard, and read many dreadful attempts at first-person narrative preaching, and nearly all of them were the result of entering into a style of communication for which the preacher had little or no instruction or guidance. On the occasions when I have witnessed a masterful first-person narrative sermon, I have experienced the presence of the Holy Spirit in ways that my little record player could never provide. I still remember encountering Simon of Cyrene in the sanctuary of Marsh Chapel at Boston University. The preacher became the man who carried Jesus's cross. I felt his reluctance, I felt his fear, it seemed as though I could see the sweat from his brow—by the end, I felt compelled to carry the cross of Christ, just as Simon had.

Congregational Apprehension

Reluctance to accept first-person narrative preaching as an effective form of sermon delivery is often held by congregations as well as pastors. The congregation that initially welcomes a first-person narrative sermon from its pastor may quickly tire of this sermon form if it becomes a staple of the Sunday morning liturgical diet. Initially, the congregation appreciates their pastor's attempt to creatively embody a biblical character. In fact, more often than not, the effort at first-person narrative sermons can be a welcome change from the typically lackluster preaching the congregants may be accustomed to hearing from their pastor. Thinking that *anything* that breaks up the monotony of the Sunday sermon is positive, parishioners gush with praise at their pastor's new and creative approach to the sermon moment. The pastor, seizing on the apparent enthusiasm of his or her people, begins to employ the use of first-person narrative preaching on a more regular basis. In

21

short order, the novelty of this approach wears off, and the congregation soon realizes that a first-person narrative sermon is just a repackaging of their pastor's poorly crafted and poorly delivered homiletical efforts.

One reason that parishioners can quickly tire of poorly crafted first-person narrative sermons is that they are all accustomed to excellence in storytelling. Everyone, even the youngest child in the congregation, is immersed in professional storytelling every day. From children's books to feature films, from daytime television to the evening news—not to mention the best sellers that make their homes on our coffee table and nightstands—well-told and professionally crafted stories touch our lives at every turn. We have an entire industry built on capturing our attention with story. The entertainment industry in America, one of the most powerful and successful industries in our country and in our world, focuses its energy and ability on creating and telling excellent stories. Actors, writers, directors, and producers spend years studying and practicing the craft of storytelling until they have it mastered.

As a result, whether we are reading *Goodnight Moon* to our children before bed or watching the nightly news ourselves, we are being conditioned to expect excellence in storytelling. So, on the very first Sunday a pastor attempts to deliver a first-person narrative sermon, the congregation will likely greet the effort warmly and praise the pastor's creativity. The second time a pastor takes on a biblical character in an attempt to communicate a biblical concept and story, that pastor better have prepared for that moment just like Dustin Hoffman or Meryl Streep would prepare for a performance. Fair or not, if clergypeople intend on entering the world of dramatic monologue, then they have to be aware that the people in their pews are well acquainted with the best of dramatic monologue. While clergy may have the corner on the market on looking at scripture and finding angles for how that text should be applied to life, professional storytellers from Mike Wallace to Meryl Streep have mastered the art of dramatic monologue. A congregation's long-term acceptance and engagement with a first-person narrative sermon style will ultimately depend on the preacher's mastery of dramatic monologue.

First-Person Narrative Preaching as Dramatic Monologue

Dramatic monologue is the term used by professional storytellers to describe that moment when an individual begins to tell a story without the help of other actors or performers. Dramatic dialogue refers to conversation that occurs between actors or performers within a story. There are rules that govern effective dramatic monologue and dialogue. And while there are precious few resources published to teach pastors how to effectively create and deliver first-person narrative sermons, there are mountains of resources designed to help would-be storytellers and actors craft and deliver dramatic monologues. There isn't a performer in film or on television who didn't begin their career by preparing and delivering dramatic monologues. Creating, preparing, and delivering dramatic monologues is *the* staple of the auditioning actor's life. Therefore, every drama bookstore across America is filled with volumes of books that help to train, teach, and equip actors who need to regularly deliver dramatic monologues with excellence. It is my belief that preachers who are willing to explore these vast resources, and are willing to approach first-person narrative sermons as dramatic monologues, will have the opportunity to master a style of storytelling that will mesmerize their parishioners and help their congregants to access, understand, and *remember* the word of God.

Preachers who master the art of dramatic monologue find it to be a deeply moving and powerful vehicle for communicating the gospel of Jesus Christ. It has the unique ability to capture the hearts, minds, and spirits of people both young and old. To effectively create and deliver first-person narrative sermons, however, a preacher must master the unique characteristics of this art form. First-person narrative sermons cannot be perceived as an opportunity to reduce the important and challenging work of exegesis. Nor is it an opportunity to be careless or overly casual in the rehearsal and delivery of the message. First-person narrative preaching is not an opportunity to be creative at the expense of working diligently to communicate a biblical concept to Christ's gathered people. First-person narrative preaching offers us a unique opportunity to blend biblical truth with a refreshingly engaging style of delivery. This may be the most time-consuming and demanding type of sermon to create and deliver, but it may also be one of the most important and effective sermon styles a pastor can learn to master. Not only that, but the individual who is committed to sound exegetical work and who can understand and employ the basic principles of dramatic monologue will have loads of fun. At its best, first-person narrative preaching is a powerful, moving, memorable, and *highly enjoyable* homiletical experience for both preachers and parishioners.

Throughout this volume you will be given tools and tips for crafting and delivering first-person narrative sermons with confidence and excellence. You will be able to get into character while getting your people into the Word of God. In a very real way, you will allow the Word to become flesh—your flesh—and that Word will powerfully and memorably dwell with your people.

2

Understanding
Dramatic Monologue

Show and Tell

Even the casual moviegoer can see that films are stories told in pictures. In film and on television, the visual image is regularly the most important aspect of the storytelling process. If you were to venture into the theater today, you would tend to notice the opposite: theatrical stage productions are stories told with words. As we prepare to explore first-person narrative preaching as dramatic monologue, it is important to note that *theater* will be the best dramatic venue to inform us. Indeed, plays, play scripts, and books and workshops that focus on creating and delivering dramatic monologues can be most helpful. With that said, even within the film and television media, there are times when dramatic monologue is employed, proving that words can still be every bit as important as pictures.

While body language, gesturing, and facial expressions can tell us a lot about a character in a given moment, the spoken word is still the most revealing form of communication. Now, of course, the spoken word can be used for false revelation. Words are used to tell lies and to disseminate misinformation to people. But when it is time for a character to open up and reveal what is really in his or her heart, dramatic monologue is readily employed. Dramatic monologue is that moment when a character has the stage—or the camera angle—all to themselves. All focus is on them. The character speaks for an extended time, revealing their secret thoughts and emotions that have been lying under the surface. It is during dramatic monologues that the audience finally begins to understand why a particular character has been acting in a particular way. By its nature a dramatic monologue reveals hidden thoughts, motives, and feelings. In movies and in plays, dramatic monologue is often employed toward the end of a story. It is true that sometimes a narrative monologue can run throughout a dramatic production, but today, typically, dramatic monologue is employed at or near the climax of a drama when motives and meanings need to be explained. Some of our greatest examples of dramatic monologue come from theatrical productions of the distant past, when audiences had a longer and more easily sustained attention span. The Greek playwrights, Shakespeare, and even some of the dramatists of the early twentieth century were masters of dramatic monologue. In ancient Greek drama, in Elizabethan theater, and even in modern drama of the first half of the twentieth century, dramatic monologues were used throughout a dramatic production. To this day, classical actors are expected to always have several Shakespearean monologues performance-ready for audition purposes.

Shakespeare's Monologues

We will take some time now to look at a couple of monologues from a classic play that is driven by extraordinary dramatic monologues. Shakespeare's *Hamlet* has some of the most memorable and compelling monologues in all of English literature. In the third act of the play, Hamlet employs some traveling actors to enact a drama intended to confirm Hamlet's suspicions that his Uncle Claudius poisoned his father in order to inherit the kingdom of Denmark and thus take Hamlet's mother (Queen Gertrude) as his bride. Up to this point, Hamlet has been driven by his suspicions, as well as by a late-night revelation of this evil deed, made to him by his father's ghost. Hamlet is filled with angst, anger, and misgivings, and he needs some more concrete proof of his uncle's villainy before he can take his revenge. The staged play, a veiled reenactment of the murder of Hamlet's father, draws a horrified response from Claudius. In Hamlet's mind, he has the proof he needs, and now he begins to look for an opportunity to exact his revenge. Claudius is utterly undone with the knowledge that his crimes are known and have been dramatized for all his court to see. To this point, Hamlet has seemed to be a waffling, weak, spiritually frustrated prince who is unable to act decisively. At the same time, Claudius appears to be a heartless villain who will stop at nothing to achieve his aims. These perceptions collide in a moment of intense and revelatory dramatic monologue within the chapel of the king's castle. Claudius begins to pray, and Hamlet discovers him alone and vulnerable. See how these two intertwined monologues work to reveal aspects of the respective characters while powerfully furthering the story and plotline:

> **King:** O my offense is rank, it smells to heaven.
> It hath the primal eldest curse upon't.

27

A brother's murder. Pray can I not,
Though inclination be as sharp as will;
My stronger guilt defeats my strong intent,
And, like a man to double business bound,
I stand in pause where I shall first begin,
And both neglect. What if this cursed hand
Were thicker than itself with brother's blood,
Is there not rain enough in the sweet heavens
To wash it white as snow?

Immediately, we realize that it was not fear that drove the king from the play, but guilt. Dramatic monologues always reveal something about the character speaking, as well as about the story of which the character is a part. Here we see that Claudius is racked by guilt, not fear. In fact, he is so guilt-ridden he can't even pray. And we learn that however evil and ugly Claudius's deeds are, he clearly desires forgiveness. He is not merely a mindless, heartless brute. Quite the contrary: Claudius is as deeply conflicted as his young nephew.

> **King:** . . . But O, what form of prayer
> Can serve my turn? "Forgive me my foul
> murder?"
> That cannot be, since I am still possess'd
> Of those effects for which I did the murder—
> My crown, mine own ambition, and my queen.
> May one be pardon'd and retain the offense?

Again, it is confirmed that Claudius has indeed been considering the deep and troubling consequences of his actions. In this monologue, the audience sees the king's humanity in all its disturbing manifestations. The monologue is particularly effective because of the inherent tension and conflict that is present in it. The king desires forgiveness, but he has no intention of giving up the rewards of his evil deeds. He has his kingdom and his wife; his ambitions have been achieved. Is there any way he can receive forgiveness without repentance? This monologue works because it draws the audience into a very real human conflict. The very best dramatic monologues always possess some form of tension and conflict within them.

> **King:** In the corrupted currents of this world
> Offense's gilded hand may shove by justice,
> And oft 'tis seen the wicked prize itself
> Buys out the law. But 'tis not so above:
> There is no shuffling, there the action lies
> In his true nature, and we ourselves compell'd
> Even to the teeth and forehead of our faults
> To give in evidence. What then? What rests?
> Try what repentance can. What can it not?
> Yet what can it when one can not repent?

It is also important to notice that Shakespeare, like any competent playwright, always keeps Claudius "in character." Claudius is not addressing the audience here, there is no anachronism, and there isn't a word uttered that seems "out of character." I will say more about this in later chapters, but many of the most basic failings in first-person narrative sermons occur because the preacher doesn't remain "in character." To be "in character," as opposed to being "out of character," means that the actor playing Claudius must always act, speak, and move *as Claudius* would act, speak, and move. You may notice a significant difference between the film versions of Mel Gibson's Hamlet and Kenneth Branagh's Hamlet. In the former, you see traces of Mel Gibson's personality that have been evident in his body of work from *Mad Max* and *Lethal Weapon*, while you see little or nothing of Kenneth Branagh in his portrayal of Hamlet. It is painful to watch and hear a preacher take on the role of Solomon only to speak directly to the audience, and

29

then talk to them about everything from *New York Times* editorials to UFO sightings, while speaking just as he or she would during a pastoral care session. In the two monologues we are examining, you never hear Claudius or Hamlet utter a misplaced word or phrase. They are always uncle and nephew, king and prince, murderer and revenge seeker, set squarely in the kingdom of Denmark in the sixteenth century. Claudius and Hamlet never leave the dramatic boundaries of time, place, and character. Preachers would be well served to observe these same boundaries when crafting and delivering first-person narrative sermons.

> **King:**   . . . Help, angels! Make assay.
> Bow, stubborn knees, and heart with strings of
>   steel
> Be soft as sinews of the new-born babe.
> All may be well.

The king tries desperately to enter into prayer. He does all he can to humble himself and offer his confession. Enter Hamlet. What will he do? Is his resolve firm? Will he finally act? Hamlet raises his dagger and approaches Claudius, who is now kneeling before him.

> **Hamlet:**   Now might I do it pat, now he is praying.
> And now I'll do't. And so he goes to heaven;
> And so I am revenged. That would be
>   scann'd:
> A villain kills my father, and for that,
> I, his sole son, do this same villain send
> To heaven.

Hamlet is just about to strike with his dagger and avenge his father's death when he decides there is a problem. Claudius is praying, and Hamlet fears that killing his uncle during a prayer will only ensure Claudius an eternal reward. Can revenge be genuine if the villain gets a saint's reward? In this moment of indecision, the audience gets further insight into the character and person of this conflicted prince. Again Hamlet hesitates, making the audience wonder whether this prince will ever be able to translate intention into action. We also learn more about the depth of responsibility Hamlet feels toward his father. Hamlet is his father's *only* son. If Hamlet fails, or if he fails to exact the appropriate punishment, there will be no one left to honor his father with revenge.

Hamlet: O, this is hire and salary, not revenge.
He took my father grossly, full of bread,
With all his crimes broad blown, as flush as May;
And how his audit stands who knows save heaven?
But in our circumstance and course of thought,
'Tis heavy with him. And am I then revenged,
To take him in the purging of his soul,
When he is fit and season'd for his passage?

In this section we learn more about Hamlet's concern over his father's otherworldly state. Hamlet believes it is possible that his father stands condemned for his own evil actions and thus is forced to walk the earth at night in ghostly form. Hamlet then lets the audience know that appropriate revenge will be possible only when he takes his uncle's life when Claudius's own crimes have gone unconfessed and unpardoned, not while he kneels before God.

Hamlet: No.
Up, sword, and know thou a more horrid bent.
When he is drunk asleep, or in his rage,

31

Or in the incestuous pleasure of his bed,
At game, aswearing, or about some act
That has no relish of salvation in't.
Then trip him, that his heels may kick at
    heaven
And that his soul may be as damned and
    black
As hell, whereto it goes.

Hamlet lets the audience know under what circumstances he will take Claudius's life. This section of dramatic monologue furthers the story line by offering us clues to Hamlet's future actions. By the end of this passage, we are given to believe that Hamlet will indeed act when Claudius is sin-bound. Our anticipation of the upcoming scenes of this unfolding story are heightened by the specific intentions that Hamlet has verbally shared, as well as the reality that, once again, he has hesitated to act. The audience is pushed a bit further to the edge of their seats. This dramatic monologue has revealed much about Hamlet's character and motivation, and it has also effectively revealed the unfolding story line.

King: My words fly up, my thoughts remain below.
Words without thoughts never to heaven go.

This section of dramatic monologue ends with a confession. Claudius cannot pray. He cannot make confession to God. His actions have already condemned him; now it is only a matter of time before fortune turns on him.

Advancing the Plot

Dramatic monologues always reveal a lot about the internal motivations of a character, but a monologue is dramatically effective only when it also furthers the plot and story line. There must be a point or purpose to the monologue. While it is not a hard-and-fast rule, dramatic monologues should do more than just reveal character motivation; they should push the entire story line forward. Dramatic monologues are effective theatrical devices when they reveal character *and* advance the plot.

The chapel monologues in *Hamlet* accomplish both of these aims with extreme effectiveness. We learn Claudius longs to repent but is unable to. We learn that Hamlet longs to avenge his father but must wait for the right moment. These character revelations help to heighten the dramatic tension and conflict, while at the same time furthering the plot by preparing the audience for a climactic showdown between Claudius and Hamlet at the end of the play.

Professional playwrights and screenwriters never have their characters speak just to speak. There is always a dramatic motivation or purpose behind their words. This is what makes the study of dramatic monologue so helpful to preachers who wish to craft and deliver effective first-person narrative sermons. Sermons are crafted to convey a point, as are dramatic monologues. It is important to note that dramatic monologues that have been crafted by truly talented dramatists are able to get their point across powerfully and *subtly*. If a character speaks directly to the point the dramatist is trying to make with his or her work, the work itself is often referred to as being "preachy." Being "preachy" is what every serious dramatist seeks to avoid. First-person narrative sermons have the wonderful potential of effectively communicating a point or biblical concept without becoming "preachy." That is exactly what this volume is intended to equip preachers to do.

Further Examples of Dramatic Monologue

We will now briefly examine two other monologues that will help preachers to get a better understanding of how dramatic monologues can function when they are well crafted. The first is a monologue from David Hare's Broadway hit *Racing Demon*. In this play David Hare explores some of the theological and political tensions within the Anglican church. Hare effectively pits the dying liberal arm of the church against the vibrant and jarringly evangelical branch of the church. He also wonderfully illustrates the tension between older clergy, who have settled into comfortable and well-worn patterns of church life, and the enthusiastically frustrated younger clergy, who long to help create a much more lively and dynamic church.

In the characters of Lionel and Tony, Hare masterfully pits liberal and conservative clergy and their competing visions for ministry against each other. Lionel is the seasoned, careful, and tired clerical veteran, while Tony is the young, overly confident buck who winds up challenging Lionel's ministry. As the tension between Lionel's and Tony's visions for ministry heighten, and as Lionel's ministry is directly challenged and threatened by Tony, Hare inserts a wonderful dramatic monologue that furthers the plot, while making a point and adding a laugh or two that releases some of the tension. Enter the Reverend Donald Bacon, known to his congregation and colleagues as Streaky. Streaky is a bumbling and jovial cleric who finds himself smack-dab in the middle of Tony's and Lionel's theological and ministerial wrangling. Streaky begins his prayer, which turns out to be a loose and flowing conversation with God.

Streaky: Drunk, Lord, drunk. And blissfully happy. Can't help it. Love the job. Love my work. Look at other people

34

in total bewilderment. I got to drink at the Savoy. It was wonderful. It's all wonderful. Why can't people enjoy what they have? Is it just a matter of temperament? I mean, I'm a happy priest. Always have been. Ever since I got my first job as curate at St. Anselm's, Cheam, because they needed a light tenor for the parochial Gilbert and Sullivan society. Matins, a sung Eucharist, two Evensongs, and *Iolanthe* five nights a week. It was bliss. I loved it. I tried to start it here. But there is something deep in the Jamaican character that can't find its way through *Pirates of Penzance*. It's still bliss, though. They are blissful people. Once a year we take a coach out to the sea. On the way down we have rum and curried goat. Lord, there is no end to your goodness. Then we have rum and curried goat on the way back. Lord, I have no theology. Can't do it. By my bed, there is a pile of paperbacks called *The Meaning of Meaning*, and *How to Ask Why*. They've been there for years. The whole thing's so clear. You're there. In people's happiness. Tonight, in the taste of that drink. Or the love of my friends. The whole thing's so simple. Infinitely loving. Why do people find it so hard?

This is a fantastic monologue from a truly fine playwright. In this monologue, David Hare reveals character and through that character furthers the story line while making a point. In fact, I believe Hare is preaching here, but he never gets "preachy." Through this monologue we are drawn in by the affable and simple character of Streaky. We like him. The audience can relate to him. Streaky loves people but has little capacity for systematic theology. Streaky is able to understand the basic goodness of God and cannot understand the basic meanness of people. This monologue is placed in such a way that the tension between Lionel and Tony (which is representative of a wider tension in the Anglican church) is shown for what it is: careless and foolish. And a point is clearly made: we are called by God to love one another.

In Streaky's dramatic monologue, Hare preaches the Great Commandment clearly and creatively. If only our weekly sermons were so engaging and effective. In fact, this dramatic monologue comes as close to being a first-person narrative sermon as any I have ever seen or read. Character is revealed, plot is furthered, and a point is made.

A final example is the remarkable, yet brief, dramatic monologue at the end of Yasmina Reza's play *Art*. This play takes on the ever contentious and eternal debate about what truly constitutes "art," and how friendship is as challenging and fragile as life itself. The play begins with an introductory note from Marc.

> **Marc:** My friend Serge has bought a painting. It is a canvas about five foot by four: white. The background is white and if you screw up your eyes, you can make out some fine white diagonal lines. Serge is one of my oldest friends. He's doing well for himself, he's a dermatologist and he's keen on *art*. On Monday I went to see the painting; Serge had actually got hold of it on Saturday, but he's been lusting after it for several months. This white painting with white lines.

What ensues is an entire play in which three friends bicker, belittle, challenge, critique, and express affection for one another. The "white painting" is a foil for exploring the intertwining and contentious relationships of Marc, Serge, and their spineless friend Yvan. At the outset of the play, Marc finds out that Serge paid nearly $40,000 for this white painting, and from then on, the argument cascades downhill like an avalanche. Marc thinks the painting is ridiculous, and Serge thinks Marc is being smug about artistic endeavors beyond his comprehension. Yvan, struggling with his own personal affairs, is simply brought to tears. The climax of the play comes as Marc takes a felt-tip pen and, with Serge's frustrated encouragement, draws a diagonal line across the painting, and then proceeds to draw the stick figure of a skier flying down the incline. The lights fade to black. A scene later, Marc and Serge have worked to remove the marker (and the skier) from the painting, and are in the process of reconciling with each other. Marc concludes the play with the following dramatic monologue while staring at the white painting.

> **Marc:** Under the white clouds, the snow is falling. You can't see the white clouds, or the snow. Or the cold, or the white glow of the earth. A solitary man glides downhill on his skis. The snow is falling. It falls until the man disappears back into the landscape. My friend Serge, who's one of my oldest friends, has bought a painting. It's a canvas about five foot by four. It represents a man who moves across a space and disappears.

This is dramatic monologue at its best. Character is revealed, the plot is furthered, and a powerful point is made.

Of course, this brief monologue is able to accomplish all these things because there is an entire play behind it. This brief piece by itself would mean nothing to an audience. Likewise, for a first-person narrative sermon to work, a preacher needs more than a single disconnected paragraph to do the job. With that said, this particular monologue is beautiful. After the volcanic argument between Marc and Serge that threatened their very friendship, Marc reaffirms his devotion to Serge. At the same time, he maintains his critique of the white painting with a wonderfully sarcastic wit that is in keeping with his own character development. "You can't see the white clouds, or the snow. Or the cold . . ." Marc never loses his character, even in reconciliation. Marc is Marc throughout. At the same moment of critique, Marc reveals the emphasis or point of the entire play. Referring to the previously vanished stick-figure skier, Marc says that the painting represents "a man who moves across a space and disappears." The point is powerful and universal. All things pass away; the meaning of art, art fads, friendships, arguments, and life itself. Reconciled friendship is more important than making a point when life is so short. This monologue is clean, crisp, and profound. A well-crafted first-person narrative sermon that wrapped up with a final paragraph of monologue like this would be remembered by parishioners for years to come.

3

Using Dramatic Monologue and Dialogue

Taking On the Voice of Another

As I have already suggested, taking on the voice of a biblical character to convey a biblical message to a congregation can be a very effective sermonic device. There are challenges, to be sure, but taking on the voice of another person can be an important and creative way to engage a congregation. There is no question that weekly sermon preparation and delivery is a demanding and sometimes tedious process. Preachers certainly fall into ruts, and our sermonic style can become downright predictable for our congregations. As preachers, one of our greatest challenges is to capture and then to keep the attention of our people. This does not mean we have to become entertainers, but we must always realize that the attention span of our people is short. In fact, an individual's attention span may shift every several seconds. A parishioner may be listening to us one moment, and then mentally organizing his or her grocery list the next. This means that if we want to clearly and effectively share a biblical concept with our congregations, we must be aware that part of our job is to keep their attention. First-person monologue and *dialogue* (of which I will say more later) can serve as effective communication tools if they are used skillfully and sparingly. A weekly diet of first-person narrative sermons can become as mundane as a weekly dose of sermons that have three points and end with a Shakespearean sonnet. The idea is to mix things up, to throw the congregation different pitches to keep them on their toes. If your congregation doesn't know how you are going to sermonically approach them in a given week, and you surprise them with a first-person narrative sermon, you will automatically have their attention—at least for the first few moments of your sermon.

We always need to remember that we can have the most compelling biblical point in the world, but our congregants will not care, they will not hear it, and they will certainly not remember it if we do not grab and maintain their attention. Long gone are the days when tens of thousands of people would sit on a hilltop or in a church and listen raptly to John Wesley, George Whitefield, or Henry Ward Beecher preach for hours on end. As preachers, we need not only to extract a compelling biblical idea from scripture to share with our people, but also to find creative ways to convey that concept so that our people will pay attention to it and, ideally, remember it and apply it to their daily lives. It is a daunting and sometimes frustrating task, but it is the task the Holy Spirit has set before us, and first-person narrative preaching can be a powerful ally in this effort.

Character Selection

If a preacher is going to attempt to take on the voice of another, the first step is to identify the character to be portrayed. In a sense, the sky is the limit. Preachers have chosen biblical characters, historical figures, imaginary people, and even an occasional ark animal as the mouthpiece for their first-person narrative sermon. There is, of course, always the pastor who decides to use the nearly clichéd device of dressing up as a homeless person and sitting outside the church until the opening hymn, only to address their congregation as a homeless person throughout the entire service, including the preaching moment. While I am not without opinion on the issue of character selection, I confess that very effective first-person narrative sermons have been preached through a vast array of characters. Ultimately, the individual preacher must make his or her own decision about which character to portray. With that said, my overwhelming preference is for preachers to stick exclusively to *biblical* characters. Ideally, *human* biblical characters. Telling the story of Noah and the ark from the perspective of one of the two giraffes might be cute for a children's message, but it will have little lasting impact on a mature audience of believers.

Generally speaking, many (if not most) of our people suffer from some degree of biblical illiteracy. They are simply not all that familiar with the Bible. In fact, many clergy are biblically illiterate, as well. We don't know the stories, and we don't know the characters. Taking on the character of Abraham Lincoln, or Rosa Parks, or Christopher Columbus may be very interesting for your congregation, but it will not necessarily help them to wrestle with the biblical text in all its creative power. Using the Bible and biblical characters as the basis for all of your first-person narrative preaching will help you

41

and your congregation become more familiar with the Bible and the motivations of biblical characters.

Personally, I have found it quite rewarding to study the motivations, actions, and history of a particular biblical character in preparation for a first-person narrative sermon. Exploring the intentions of David, or Peter, or Paul has served as some of the most meaningful and deep time of biblical study in my own ministry. What filled Stephen with such boldness? What compelled Ruth to want to stay with Naomi? How did Paul's prior life as Saul affect his ministry in prison? There are so many wonderful and exciting questions to be asked and answered when you begin to work with biblical characters. Those questions and answers can bring you and your people into more intimate relationship with the Word of God. And because the task of preaching is always to bring people deeply into the Word, I would suggest that you stay in the Word and utilize the characters of the Word as your primary sources for first-person narratives.

Selection Options

So how do you select a character? There may be a character that you are particularly drawn to, so this answer may come easily. You may want to take on the character of Mary, or Joseph, or even Moses. But what do you do if you have no idea what character would be best to portray? What if you are a lectionary preacher? How do you make this selection? Let's look at a particular example. Say your scripture is the story of the prodigal son (Luke 15:11–31). Read the story and on a piece of paper start to make a list of all the characters that appear in the story. List them in order of appearance. There are the obvious choices, of course: the characters around whom the story revolves. There is the father, the younger brother, and the older brother. Then there is a second tier of characters who are not central to the story but are mentioned in it. There is the citizen of the neighboring country who hires the younger son to work with his pigs, and there are the father's servants who prepare the celebration upon the younger son's return. Then there is a final tier of characters hinted at by the story's progression. These are the characters who encountered the younger son while he wasted his money living wildly in a foreign land (we must assume he handed his money over to someone for something), as well as the partygoers and the older brother's friends who are referred to at the end of the story. The only other living things that are mentioned in the story are the pigs the younger son is hired to feed, and the calf to be slaughtered for the celebration. While I have had colleagues that have suggested it might be fun to take on the role of livestock, unless you are a child playing a lamb in the Christmas pageant, I would *strongly* suggest against it! Yes, it is possible to construct other relationships and people who might have possibly factored into this story—the father must have talked to friends and neighbors, perhaps there were other servants that worked with the pigs—but that would begin to stretch far beyond the bounds of the story as the Holy Spirit has seen fit to pass it on to us.

Now that you have a fairly complete list of characters, which character do you choose as the focus of your first-person narrative? It is always best to choose characters who are well grounded in the story. You should choose the father over the imaginary innkeeper, bartender, or prostitute that the younger son might have encountered in the foreign land. The more biblical information you have about a character, the more full and true your depiction can be. From the story, we know far more about the father than we do about the older brother's friends; therefore, we will have more information with which to flesh out the character of the father than we would ever have with the friends.

With that said, it is sometimes clever to choose a more tangential character who is able to view the entire drama from a distance. The father and two brothers will naturally have intense feelings about the events that have taken place, whereas the foreign citizen who hired the younger son to tend pigs could unemotionally and somewhat objectively reflect on the entire story. Bear in mind, however, that choosing a character that is not even mentioned in the text (an innkeeper or a bartender) can be dangerous. First, it takes you and your people out of the Bible. Second, if you feel free to create characters, you are already taking a step toward re-creating the story to suit your own purposes, which are not necessarily the purposes of the text itself. First-person narrative preaching should never be used as an opportunity for creativity to overstep scriptural integrity. First-person narrative preaching can and should be a fun and creative experience, but never at the cost of the message that the scripture was written to impart.

There are, of course, several other characters that are not mentioned in the story of the prodigal son that a preacher might want to consider as potential subjects for a first-person narrative sermon. As Jesus is telling this story, the disciples are sitting around him, as are the tax collectors and the Pharisees who are mentioned in the beginning of chapter 15. We can also assume that there is a great crowd of people from across the Galilean countryside. Jesus is telling this story in an attempt to confront the Pharisees' narrow and exclusive view of who is acceptable in the sight of God. The Pharisees are the older brother refusing to come to the party, and the tax collectors and sinners are the younger brother who is joyously embraced by his father.

Parables offer a wonderful array of characters on which a preacher can base a first-person narrative sermon. The sermon can be shared by a character in the story, or even someone listening to the story. The message of this parable could certainly be told by a Pharisee, or a disciple, or one of the Galilean peasants who were following Jesus from town to town. All of these are acceptable characters from which to choose. In our attempt to help our people learn and understand the biblical story, however, it is still always a good idea to choose a character for whom we have a fairly solid history and description. If you decide to tell this story through the voice and person of one of the disciples, which one do you choose? We know more about the character of Peter than we do about Andrew; we know more about the characters of James and John than we do about Thaddeus; we know more about Thomas than we do about Simon the Zealot. Therefore, in my opinion and experience, Peter, James, John, or Thomas would be better choices for first-person narrative sermons than Andrew, Thaddeus, or Simon. The more we know about a character, the more effectively and accurately we will be able to portray them to our congregations. We know more about Pharisees than we do about the people who followed Jesus throughout the Judean countryside. Always try to choose characters you will be able to do further research on in the biblical text; it will be a boon to your sermon preparation and to your congregation who may know little or nothing about what and who a Pharisee is.

Using Dialogue in the Preaching Moment

There is another dramatic device that is similar to dramatic monologue, which is worth mentioning at this point, even though it is not the primary focus of this text.

First-person narrative sermons are a way of sharing a biblical idea or concept through the voice of someone else. Likewise, dramatic monologue and *dialogue* can be used within a traditional deductive or inductive sermon. The Bible is full of stories, monologues, poetry, and ordinances, as well as dialogue between two or more characters. The Bible is a richly textured book, and our sermons should be every bit as textured. If the Bible includes dramatic monologue and dialogue, why shouldn't our sermons utilize these dramatic techniques as well? I would encourage you to use dramatic monologue and dialogue often in the body of your sermons. If you are telling a story or offering an illustration about a conversation you overheard while pumping gas at the local gas station, take on the characters of the people you overheard, and share that conversation with your congregation using *their* words. If you are preaching on Paul's sermon to the Athenians, share a bit of dramatic monologue—speak as Paul, and let your congregation know some of what he was thinking as he spoke at the Acropolis.

Remember, we are always trying to maintain the attention of our congregation, so use as many techniques as you can to *command* their attention. Don't just tell the story of the faith the Pilgrims must have had when they suffered their way through their first winter in the New World. Use the words you imagine they would have used at the time. Imagine the questions those sick and weary travelers would have had for William Bradford: *"Did you bring us out of persecution in Europe, so that we could die in this wilderness?"* And how would Bradford have responded? *"The Lord didn't call us here to die. Christ has called us here to live!"* Only to have the Pilgrims respond by saying, *"Look at us—we're dying—when can we start living?"*

I would encourage every preacher to regularly use moments of dramatic monologue and dialogue within most of their sermons. If you have a red-letter edition of the Bible, you will notice that all the red represents monologue or dialogue. If the Holy Spirit saw fit to include all that monologue and dialogue in our sacred text, perhaps we could allow that same Spirit to similarly enliven our weekly sermons.

4

Studying Character

A Character Chosen

You have chosen your biblical story, or rather, stories. It is Christmas Eve, and you will be working with the combined birth narratives of Matthew and Luke. You plan to harmonize the two accounts, knowing that each birth narrative is distinctly different and resists blending. But it is Christmas Eve, after all, and what would the evening be without all the beloved characters—the angels, shepherds, wise men, a pensive Joseph, and a faithfully expectant Mary? As the livestock graze about the manger, Joseph is questioning his motives, while Mary is treasuring all the evening's events in her heart. Biblical inaccuracy aside, Christmas Eve begs for a first-person narrative sermon. People who rarely attend church will be seated before you on this particular evening. These C&E Christians will carry with them a year's worth of expectations that, frankly, no service or sermon can meet. Only the Lord can meet them where they are and take them to where they hope to be. But you are the preacher, and you need to give it your best shot. You have to communicate with your church secretary's uncle who is visiting from California and hasn't been in church for years, as well as Mr. and Mrs. Patten, who haven't missed a service since they first claimed their seats next to the church's left-hand aisle thirty years ago. You have decided to take on the role and character of Joseph in hopes of capturing the attention and imagination of your Christmas Eve congregation.

Choosing a Moment

So, knowing whom you will portray is an important step, but now the work begins. You know who you are, that is, you know your *name* for the evening, but *where* will you be? And *when* will you be? You need to decide on the time and place of your dramatic presentation. You should note that it is advisable to pick a fairly narrow slice of time with which to work.

Long ago, great epic dramas were the norm in the theatrical world. The Greeks created vast dramas in which the heavens and the earth were either woven together or torn apart. Elizabethan drama did much the same. If you take a look sometime at a cast list from one of Shakespeare's masterworks, and set it alongside the cast list of the latest Pulitzer Prize–winning play, you will find a startling contrast. A Shakespearean play will range all over the countryside, involve peasants and kings, dabble in love and war, and end with everyone falling in love or everyone killing each other. You will see thirty or more characters parade onstage throughout the drama. You may laugh, cry, and question during a good Shakespearean romp, but in the end, you may find you have often been more entertained by the story line than by the inner motivations of the characters. Epic dramas often focus on how the outside world or outside influences impact characters. Read contemporary drama and you may find two characters sitting on a park bench dealing with their deep inner longings and hesitations for the entire length of the play. In contemporary drama, characters may not travel far, but they travel deep. The story line is often of secondary importance to the inner turmoil that is explored.

While the Bible is an epic drama with God as the central, and often tragic, character, a first-person narrative sermon will not be effective if you fail to narrow its focus. If you choose to take on the character of Abraham, Moses, or King David, you must decide where to dive in. It will be difficult, if not impossible, to stand before a congregation as Moses, overlooking the Promised Land, recalling his entire life's journey. Rather, it is best to pick one moment—the killing of the Egyptian, God speaking through the burning bush, Moses's first visit to Pharaoh, preparing for Passover, going up the mountain to speak with God, returning with the commandments and encountering the golden calf, or the people grumbling in the desert—and explore it thoroughly. Pick a day in the life of your character to portray; don't try to cram your character's entire life into one sermon. Having a well-focused homiletical idea will also help to narrow the dramatic focus of your sermon.

But remember, tonight is Christmas Eve and you are Joseph, and you need to decide *when* and *where* you are. The nature of Christmas Eve obviously makes your decision a bit easier. Any other day of the year you could select several acceptable moments in Joseph's life from which to begin your dramatic monologue. You might choose his first dream that prompts him to remain with Mary, or the moment when he learns he will have to travel to Bethlehem for the empire's census, or the dream that leads him to flee with Mary and Jesus to Egypt. But tonight is about Jesus's birth, so your decisions should be easy to make. The baby Jesus is born, and you are in Bethlehem. It is from here that you will build your narrative.

Who Are You Really?

So, you say you are Joseph, but who is Joseph anyway? How old is he? What kind of man is he? What is his vocation? Where did he grow up? Who are his parents? How did he meet Mary? What are his aspirations? What disappointments has he faced in life? It is now time to research in earnest, and the more questions you can ask and answer about your character, the more depth and power there will be to your characterization. Start reading all the passages you can find about Joseph. This will entail reading and rereading the birth narratives in both Matthew and Luke. You will also look for other references to Joseph in the gospels. As with most biblical characters, you will find it challenging to create a thorough life history of Joseph. Joseph is hardly mentioned anywhere but in the first couple of chapters of Matthew and Luke. But every reference you find that relates to your character can lend added texture to your portrayal.

In the Gospel of Mark, the people of Nazareth respond to the authority of Jesus by asking *"Is this not the carpenter and Mary's son and the brother of James and Joses and Judas and Simon, and are not his sisters here with us?"* This information offers us the insight that Joseph is likely a carpenter, and that he is also a father of many other children. In the birth narratives, however, we are able to glean quite a lot of information about Joseph. In

Matthew, it is striking that it is Joseph, not Mary, who hears the announcement of the birth of Jesus. Joseph has three dreams that relate to the birth and safekeeping of Jesus. Clearly Joseph has, listens to, and acts on his dreams. Joseph is a dreamer. As you research, take time to jot down all the information you can about Joseph. Keep a running list. Joseph is a carpenter. Joseph is a dreamer. Joseph lives in Nazareth and is a descendant of David. Joseph is engaged.

As you read about Joseph you will find that there are certain aspects of his character that are more curious and interesting than other areas of his life. His life as a dreamer and as a pursuer of dreams is far more intriguing than his life as a carpenter, and, as it turns out, we have much more information about his dreams than we do about his vocation. One of the most remarkable aspects of Joseph's story is his change of heart about his engagement to Mary. When Mary tells Joseph she is pregnant, he decides to call off their marriage. However, after his dream, Joseph makes the decision to stay with Mary. We learn they travel to Bethlehem, and while they are there, Mary gives birth.

You will often find that the events and happenings in the Bible give rise to questions that you will not be able to directly answer. Make a list of questions that arise from the text, because they will likely give you flesh and spirit with which to clothe your character. How were Mary and Joseph treated after the pregnancy was discovered? How would pregnancy out of wedlock be greeted by their families, friends, and community? Did Mary and Joseph ever have doubts? Why, in the Gospel of Luke, are Mary and Joseph alone in a barn when they have traveled to Joseph's city of origin? Was there no extended family to take them in? Why is this young couple alone? How young are they? How would Mary and Joseph have responded to the shepherds who visited them that first night? Jot down each question, whether or not you find an answer to it in the biblical text.

Further Research

For the majority of biblical characters, we have little more than a few lines on which to draw out a character. In fact, many biblical characters are nothing more than a name in a genealogy. Once you have gleaned all you can from the text about your character, you need to look at other potential sources of information. Where is Nazareth? What was Bethlehem like in the first century? What was a Roman census like? Were taxes involved? Who is Quirinius? What would the social status of carpenters and shepherds have been in Palestine? What are magi?

Begin to imagine the other personalities involved in the story. Keep asking questions and write them down. Place yourself en route from Nazareth to Bethlehem. Look around. Consult Bible atlases and photo journals. What would Mary and Joseph's journey have been like? Along what route would they have traveled, and how long would the trip have taken?

Most of this information is available to the preacher who is willing to dig for it. The more information you have about your character, the more successful you will be in crafting a first-person narrative sermon.

Creative License

Even when you are portraying a biblical character whose life is well chronicled, it is nearly impossible to construct "a day in the life" without engaging your creative imagination. At best, we have only skeletal pictures

54

of biblical characters, so any and every first-person narrative sermon requires some creative license. The best and most convincing of actors in film and theater get a script for a role in much the same way. They are given a "part." Their character has a name, lines, and a place within an active story line, but there are countless questions about their character that the script simply does not answer. The most accomplished of performers will delve deep into their character and literally create a life beyond the script. On paper they may be playing a detective that is engaged in a perplexing murder mystery. They will read the script, gather as many details as they can, and then begin to create a character inventory. This inventory will address all aspects of the character's life, even if they will never directly factor into a given performance. A character inventory includes everything from a description of the detective's childhood to what they typically eat for breakfast and where they eat it. Actors make creative decisions that help to complete the picture of the character they are portraying. While it may seem odd to "make up" seemingly insignificant details of a character's life, the process helps an actor "get into character," thus making their performance all the more believable. An actor's job is to make a particular character come to life, and that is the minister's job when we craft first-person narrative sermons.

So, the questions continue: If Joseph is a carpenter, did he learn the craft from his father? What kind of carpenters are they? Do they build homes or furniture? Was Joseph pleased with his arranged marriage to Mary? Did he find Mary attractive? What does Joseph like to do in his free time? Does he have hobbies? Does he get along with his parents? You may not answer these questions within your sermon, but the answers may help you craft a more vivid picture of who Joseph might have been. I would nonetheless suggest that creative license be limited to the world of the text. King David would not have had a cell phone. Esther would not have worn sunglasses. And Peter would not have picked up a copy of the *New York Times* on the way to his boat. As soon as a preacher allows himself or herself to get cute and include present-day props or images to enter the biblical life of a character, he or she begins to substitute low-brow entertainment for the transformative power of biblical education. When crafting a first-person narrative sermon, feel free to get creative, but resist the temptation to get cute.

Making a Point

Now, whether it is a narrative, a first-person narrative, a deductive sermon, or an inductive sermon, to be truly effective every message must convey a biblical concept or a homiletical idea. The biblical writers were not just telling stories. Biblical authors were not merely beat reporters looking to relate the facts to impartial observers. These ancient writers were intent on making points and communicating principles of faith.

As preachers, our job is virtually the same. We take a biblical passage, we try to distill the message the author was attempting to convey, and then we try to relate that idea or teaching to a particular congregation gathered in a specific place and moment in time. First-person narrative sermons are not simply storytelling opportunities. We are not telling a story and then leaving the interpretation up to the congregation. First-person narratives must have a clear point to be delivered. Before pen is put to paper, or a single letter is typed on a keyboard, a preacher must be clear about what a biblical text is trying to say.

A preacher must complete all the good homiletical work that would be done normally in the course of sermon preparation. You should never even begin to craft a message until you feel confident that you have a solid handle on the biblical concept the writer intended to convey. There are countless volumes on sermon construction that can help novice preachers and seasoned homileticians distill the themes and ideas of biblical text. Every preacher must approach exegetical work with great earnestness, so as not to distort the biblical message within the pages of our holy text. Conveying a biblical idea to a gathered congregation should be a preacher's commitment in every sermon, no matter the homiletical style chosen to deliver it.

An Example: Joseph

What follows is an example of a first-person narrative sermon that is the result of biblical research and creative imagination. In it, you can witness the blending of biblical fidelity and thoughtful creativity. A biblical concept is clearly conveyed, and the integrity of character, time, and place is never compromised. The sermon is void of any anachronism, and there are no careless attempts to establish a cheap rapport with the contemporary audience. We meet Joseph on Christmas Eve:

> I am here because of a dream . . . though dreams have a way of fading from my mind. At one moment the dream is so vivid, and then in the next . . . the dream vanishes like mist. I've doubted so many times . . . was I doing the right thing? Was it worth all the trouble—all the grief? How much faith can you put in a dream, anyway? But, my God, it is true. It is real. Mary handed him to me, saying, *"Joseph, this is God's child, but he is your son."* He is so tiny . . . so beautiful, fragile. I was afraid I would drop him—I've never held a baby before—never wanted to before. I looked at him—his tiny little hands

57

and feet—and said, *"Your name is Jesus . . . you are God's child, but you are my son."* Already I love him . . . all because of a dream.

My mother always said I was a dreamer, and my father said that is exactly what concerned him. My father, Jacob, is a carpenter. He builds homes for people to live in. *"Meaningful work,"* he calls it, *"God's work . . . building other people homes."* As his apprentice I learned the craft, but my heart was never in it. I liked to build furniture. Our dining table. A bench. A chair. A footstool. My father called it a waste of time. *"People won't buy a table or chair unless they have a house to set them in. You'll never make a living at that."* I began to work by my father's side less frequently after that. I spent more time with my friends and dabbling in the building of chairs. I would carve the backrests and armrests—inlaying symbols and images with olive wood into the seats. It could take me weeks to finish a single piece. My father would say, *"Who are you making that for, a prince?"* One day I got angry with him and said, *"When you are dead and gone, all you will leave behind are some tiny houses in this godforsaken town of Nazareth, while my furniture will be used by kings and princes and governors throughout the empire."* No father should ever have his son speak to him like that. My mother tried to calm his anger. *"Let Joseph have his dreams,"* she said. *"He's only a boy."*

It wasn't long after that when my father sat me down and said, *"Joseph, you've got a choice to make in life. You can either be a dreamer, or you can pursue a dream. You can spend your life fooling around and daydreaming about all the things you wish to do, or you can get serious about doing them. You want to build furniture for kings—fine—learn the craft and excel at it."* And then he looked even more intently at me and said, *"Boys dream, Joseph; men pursue dreams. And the only dreams worth pursuing—the only dreams that are from God—are those dreams that benefit others as much as yourself."* I will never forget those words.

Mary seemed like a dream worth pursuing. Our parents decided we would become married if, after a year of engagement and courting, we felt love for each other. And I do love Mary. She is beautiful—inside and out. She is strong, in a quietly prayerful way. She has faith that puts my own to shame. She never lies, never even shades the truth. Throughout our engagement, I always looked forward to seeing her.

That is, until the day she told me she was pregnant. I was beside myself—I was furious. I remember I said things . . . I called her things . . . I was *certain* . . . she had betrayed me. Mary was pregnant, and I was not the father. How could she do this to me? Did she have any idea what people would say? I would have to live with this humiliation for the rest of my life. Mary just stood there silently. She didn't tremble, she didn't cringe at my words, she just stood there, tears streaming down her face as I continued to rant. When I was through, she said something about an angel, and that the child was God's . . . I wouldn't hear it. I left after telling her not to breathe a word of this to anyone. I needed time to think. But I couldn't—I couldn't pray, I couldn't fast—my rage consumed me. I decided to dismiss Mary, to call off the engagement . . . but I would do it quietly, for her sake and mine. She would have to handle her pregnancy on her own.

But then I had a dream. The night before I was to tell Mary I was cutting off the engagement . . . I had this dream. It seemed so real . . . it *was* real. An angel of the Lord stood at the foot of my bed and said, "*Joseph, son of David, do not be afraid to take Mary as your wife, for the child conceived in her is from the Holy Spirit. She will bear a son, and you shall name him Jesus, for he will save his people from their sins.*" Over and over I had that same dream until I woke up. "*Joseph, son of David, do not be afraid to take Mary as your wife.*" Then I heard the voice of my father. "*You can be a dreamer, or you can pursue the dream. Boys dream, men pursue dreams. And dreams that are from God benefit others as much as yourself.*"

59

That night I decided it was time to be a man. I went to Mary, I apologized, and I promised to marry her . . . no matter what.

As Mary grew with her pregnancy, I told everyone the child was mine. To have a child outside of marriage is a disgrace. Our families refused to take us in—they turned their backs on us. My friends don't speak to me anymore. Work has been hard to come by. People snicker and make jokes at our expense. At synagogue, the other men shake their heads disapprovingly in my direction. It has been difficult. On more than one occasion, I wished that I had let Mary go. But that was my will, not God's. God needed me by Mary's side.

And Mary has been extraordinary. We had to travel ninety miles from Nazareth to Bethlehem. Mary didn't complain once. Over a week we trekked over mountain ridges and through valleys . . . I would look at Mary and . . . well, she seemed to me more like an angel than a woman. I saw the strength of God in her. And tonight. Here in Bethlehem. In my hometown. With every door closed to us—all alone—Mary gave birth in a barn. She encouraged me more than I encouraged her. We wrapped the child in cloths. I gave him his name. Jesus. And then we laid him in a cattle trough so Mary could rest.

That's when the shepherds came, God bless them. Shepherds are not held in high regard here. But they have birthed so many lambs and goats, we were grateful for their care. They are with Mary now. When they arrived, they said angels had sent them to us. Angels. Angels had told them, *"To you is born this day in the city of David a Savior, who is the Messiah, the Lord. You will find the child wrapped in cloths and lying in a manger."* When Mary heard it, she looked at me, smiled, and said, *"I told you so. I told you so."*

I know. I know. God is good, that is all I can say. And my father was right. . . . You can be a dreamer, or you can pursue a dream. And God's dreams for your life will always stretch beyond your own wishes, to the well-being of others. Maybe I will never make furniture that will

60

grace the palaces of kings and princes . . . maybe I will only be remembered for this one moment in time. Perhaps I will forever be Joseph, husband of Mary—Mary, the mother of Jesus. That is where my dream has led me . . . and I believe I can live with that. What dream has God laid on your heart? Will you pursue it? It may be the very thing for which you are forever remembered.

This is a good, solid example of a first-person narrative sermon. The character seems real. The biblical integrity of the story is intact, and yet plenty of creativity has been employed. The father-and-son relationship, which is not biblical, is still in keeping with the character of Joseph and serves as a significant driving force within the narrative. The scorn Mary and Joseph encounter from their families and community helps to explain the biblical reality that this couple was left alone in Bethlehem. And the research around the social status and vocation of the shepherds helps to explain why they may have been welcomed guests that holy night. All of these details aside, the point or purpose of the sermon is clear. God grants us dreams that are meant to be pursued for the benefit of others, as much as for ourselves.

This is also a fine example of presenting a biblical character without having to make contemporary adjustments of any kind. Notice that Joseph didn't introduce himself, nor did he need anyone else to make an introduction. The preacher went directly "into character" and stayed in biblical character throughout the entire sermon. When you trust in a biblical character, the biblical story, and the words you have crafted, there is simply no need for introductions, props, costumes, anachronism, or other gimmicks. Faithfully present your congregation a biblical character and a biblical story containing a biblical point or idea, and you will have offered them a deeply moving and educational sermon experience.

5

Telling a Story

Plot Remembered

In the course of studying the character you will portray, you must never lose sight of the fact that you are telling a story. Your sermon is a narrative; therefore, it must have a beginning, a middle, and an end, and it should be driven by conflict and resolution. Your job is to tell a story with your sermon. One of the beauties of this sermon form is that it is often far easier for the preacher to remember the movements of a story than it is to remember multiple points of a sermon. However, to maintain the attention of the congregation, you must attempt to master the art of plot development.

Plot is another term for a story line. If you are watching a television program, a movie, or a theatrical production, or if you are reading a book, you will likely be able to follow a fairly clear progression of plot development. Plot is the skeleton upon which drama comes alive.

News stories, sitcoms, even *Saturday Night Live* sketches all involve plot development. Without an undergirding plot, story cannot happen. An evening newscast without stories would be nothing more than a program of information dissemination. Plot allows information to be gathered and structured into patterns that naturally engage an audience of viewers, listeners, or readers.

Developing a plot or story line is not rocket science; in fact, it is an art form that is fairly easy to learn. As long as you know the rules, structuring a basic story is fairly easy. In the formation of first-person narrative sermons, our task may be even easier because the story we are telling will likely be embedded implicitly or explicitly in the biblical text. The majority of times you craft a first-person narrative sermon, you will simply be expanding upon a biblical story—you will already have much of the skeleton in place—all you will need to do is fill in what is missing. Knowing what is missing is much easier when you have a firm handle on the essential components of plot development.

Introductions

Whether screenwriter, playwright, or novelist, every writer knows that when their manuscript finds its way into the hands of a producer or publisher, they have exactly ten pages to capture the reader's attention and imagination. If they fail in this, the manuscript is unceremoniously dropped into the circular file. Take notice of your own response the next time you go to a movie or turn on the television. Because you can channel-surf so effortlessly, your willingness to focus on a television program for an extended period of time is greatly diminished. If, however, you have just paid ten dollars for a movie ticket and another ten dollars for a small popcorn and soda, your investment is quite a bit higher. In either case, of course, you are willing to give the story a chance to captivate you. Sitting on your couch or in a theater seat, you have a deep desire to be told a good story, and so you are willing to suspend judgment for a few minutes. After that, the program or film has either sucked you in or turned you off. While you may give a movie about ten minutes before you make a judgment on its story line, your attention to the television program, no doubt, will be even shorter.

The creator of the most successful and longest-running crime drama in television history is well aware of this reality and has effectively dealt with it for years. Dick Wolf's *Law & Order* has virtually the same plot structure for every episode. The *Law & Order* opening tease and premise is simple. "In the criminal justice system, the people are represented by two separate yet equally important groups: the police who investigate crime and the district attorneys who prosecute the offenders. These are their stories." Within the first ten to twenty seconds of the opening scene, a dead body is discovered by some unsuspecting bystander. The murder is identified, and the customary dramatic tension of *Law & Order* is off and running for the next twenty minutes. (I will refer to *Law & Order* throughout this chapter, because it has such a solid, identifiable, and predictable system of plot development. More than six hundred episodes were created over the past sixteen years. Therefore, it is a dramatic series that, through syndication, can be watched nearly every hour of every day. If you want a good example of plot progression and basic storytelling, you may want to watch it.)

In your first-person narrative sermon, as is the case for all sermons, you have only a couple of minutes to captivate your listeners. All the goodwill and congregational affection you have garnered over the years will carry you only a moment or two; if you haven't drawn your congregation in after your first two minutes, they will be mentally organizing their sock drawer by minute three. So, what makes for a good introduction to a first-person narrative sermon? I encourage preachers to get their congregations off balance. Now, as long as you are not feeding your congregation a steady diet of first-person narrative sermons, the sermon form itself will initially upset your congregation's equilibrium. They expected you to deliver the sermon this morning, but instead, Moses showed up, or Mary Magdalene, or the apostle Paul! However, you can shake things up even more than that.

So often, first-person narrative sermons unfortunately begin something like this: the pastor gets up into the pulpit and greets the congregation and then begins the sermon by saying, "While I had planned on preaching a sermon to you this morning, it is my profound pleasure to extend those duties to an unexpected guest. Unbeknownst to me, Moses himself had decided to worship with us this morning, and I took the opportunity when I greeted him earlier to ask if he might say a few words to us this morning." The pastor then crudely takes on the character of Moses by saying something like, "When I woke up this morning, I didn't expect to be with you all, but God said, 'Moses, I need you to go down and talk to those folks at First Church.'" As soon as this introduction is finished, half the congregation is uncomfortable and wondering what on earth they are in for. Please, please, please avoid the temptation of making a hokey introduction of yourself as a biblical character. Instead, craft your sermon so that the realization that you are a biblical character sneaks up on the congregation and surprises them. Parishioners cannot object to that which they don't know is coming. Look again at the beginning of the Joseph sermon:

I am here because of a dream . . . though dreams have a way of fading from my mind. At one moment the dream is so vivid, and then in the next . . . the dream vanishes like mist. I've doubted so many times . . . was I doing the right thing? Was it worth all the trouble—all the grief? How much faith can you put in a dream, anyway? But, my God, it is true. It is real. Mary handed him to me, saying, *"Joseph, this is God's child, but he is your son."* He is so tiny . . . so beautiful, fragile. I was afraid I would drop him—I've never held a baby before—never wanted to before. I looked at him—his tiny little hands and feet—and said, *"Your name is Jesus . . . you are God's child, but you are my son."* Already I love him . . . all because of a dream.

This is a terrific introduction, because of the way it draws in the audience. Initially, there is this talk about dreams that everyone can relate to. There is no indication that anything is different. Pastor is being pastor. This is just a typical sermon. However, when the preacher says, *"I've doubted so many times . . . was I doing the right thing?"* the congregation's imagination is piqued. What is pastor going to say? Is this a personal confession? What are pastor's doubts? Then the focus shifts again as the preacher says, *"Mary handed him to me saying, 'Joseph, this is God's child, but he is your son.'"* Suddenly, a significant portion of the congregation is aware that something is different. Did he just call himself Joseph? What's he doing? Their curiosity is heightened even further. Finally, as the character of Joseph holds up the imaginary child and says, *"Your name is Jesus . . . you are God's child, but you are my son,"* the congregation gets it. The introduction has surprised them and grabbed their attention, and now we're off.

One of the strongest introductions you will read in chapter 11 is from the first-person narrative of Hagar, Sarai's maidservant in Genesis. This sermon was delivered by a seminary student who is a member of my congregation. The sermon begins with a wonderfully short and direct introductory sentence, *"I hate my name."* Immediately, every member of the congregation sat up on the edge of their seat wondering, Why on earth does Debbie hate her name? Debbie is a fine name. We have six or seven other Debbies in our church family. What's wrong with Debbie? Moments later, we realized the name was Hagar, and we were off! If you can grab people's attention with your introduction, you are well on your way to accomplishing the goal of every introduction—to set the scene for the rest of the narrative.

Setting the Scene

The truth is, you can grab your congregation's attention in a whole host of ways. However, getting their attention is just the first step of a successful introduction. An introduction to a first-person narrative sermon must set the scene for the entire drama. To set the scene, you must let the congregation know who you are, where you are, and where you are going. You have to paint a picture or create an image for your congregation that situates them solidly in a specific time and place.

First, you need to let people know who you are. As I mentioned previously, the more creative you are with this, the better. As soon as the congregation knows you are Joseph, they know they aren't in Kansas anymore. You can certainly choose to place your character in contemporary time. You could have Joseph address your congregation directly in their time, but that is often not as interesting as transporting your congregation back to Joseph's time. If you choose to have Joseph or another biblical character address your congregation where they are, then the need to set the scene is greatly reduced. The congregation will need to know only who you are and what your character wants to tell them. If, however, you take your congregation back to Bethlehem, you have to create an image of Bethlehem in their minds. What are the sights and smells around you? What do the buildings look like? Can you see the stars? Is it cold? Who is with you? Are there any landmarks of note?

In the above example, Joseph's introduction made the audience fully aware that he had just been holding Jesus. He makes it clear that he is a proud father with his hands still damp from holding the newly birthed infant. We get a clear image of a strong father holding his delicate and precious little son. If you are going to take on the character of Moses on the edge of the Red Sea, your introduction has to allow your congregation to see Pharaoh's armies in the distance, the Red Sea stretching to the horizon, and the present fear and frustration of the Hebrew people. If you are going to portray Ruth gathering wheat in Boaz's field, the congregation needs to see the other laborers, the sheaves of wheat that are left for Ruth, and Ruth's sweat and toil.

Once the congregation knows who you are and where you are, you need to begin to let them know where you are going. A story moves, and it needs to begin to develop in the introduction. As is true with many sermon styles, it is good not to show your hand too quickly. While you need to take your people on a journey, you don't have to tell them their destination right up front. Stories are so much more interesting when listeners don't know exactly where you are going to wind up. With that said, *you* need to be clear that you are indeed taking your people somewhere. The introduction must at least hint at the direction you are about to take.

Again, if you watch *Law & Order*, within the first few seconds you see the murder. You are introduced to the case to be solved. You don't know exactly how the story will unfold, but you know it will directly relate to the dead person on the sidewalk. In the Joseph sermon, we are immediately aware that a dream or dreams will propel the story line. What is the dream Joseph is referring to? How did a dream bring him to Bethlehem? Why and when did Joseph doubt his dream? As with all good introductions, we are given a trajectory, not a destination. We are given questions, not answers. And though we have just begun, we can't wait to see what happens next.

Obstacles and Conflict

Once the trajectory has been set, to create drama or dramatic tension there must be obstacles to overcome and conflicts to resolve. A story is always driven by obstacles that frustrate resolution. In Shakespeare's *Hamlet*, conflict and obstacles abound from the opening scenes. Hamlet is told by his father's ghost that his uncle Claudius poisoned him. Hamlet wonders if this revelation is true. The entire play is guided by Hamlet's desire to uncover the truth and, subsequently, to seek revenge. Now, a practical-minded person might simply suggest that Hamlet ask his uncle about his father's death. Did Claudius kill Hamlet's father in order to marry Gertrude? If Claudius fesses up to the murder, resolution is achieved without any excess drama. But story is propelled by drama, so Hamlet must encounter obstacles that frustrate resolution if the audience is to be drawn into the story. The very first obstacle Hamlet faces is his own doubt. How can he trust a ghost, an apparition from the underworld? Is the ghost worthy of his trust, or is the apparition bent on damning Hamlet?

Hamlet: The spirit I have seen may be a devil, and the devil hath power t'assume a pleasing shape;

70

yea, perhaps out of my own weakness and
my melancholy, as he is very potent with
such spirits, abuses me to damn me.

Hamlet cannot take revenge on his uncle until he
learns the true nature of his father's apparition. This
uncertainty serves as the first obstacle to the play's ultimate resolution. The drama is propelled forward by
many unanswered questions. How will Hamlet be able
to discern the truth of his father's death? Can he trust
the ghost? Can this waffling Danish prince topple the
powerful king of Denmark? The trajectory is clear. The
truth of Hamlet's father's death must be revealed. How
that will happen is the fuel for the entire drama.

As in so many good dramas, once an obstacle or conflict is overcome, another challenge appears, thus frustrating the resolution yet again. Once Claudius's mur-
derous treachery is revealed, the question of revenge
moves front and center. How will Hamlet avenge his
father's death? When will it take place? How will Hamlet's
mother understand his actions? The story is awash in
obstacles and conflict. Hamlet needs to gain his mother's
reluctant trust. Hamlet must avoid the murder plot the
king has laid for him. Hamlet must keep his intentions
secret, even while they are eating him up inside. Hamlet
must deal with the death of his lover, Ophelia. Subsequently, he must avoid the deadly intentions of Ophelia's
brother, Laertes. He must also decide when and how to
kill Claudius, so that he ensures his uncle's spirit de-
scends to hell instead of rising to heaven. There are, in
fact, so many obstacles and conflicts to work through
in this drama that many observers have quipped that
Shakespeare himself decided that it was easier to simply
kill everyone off in the end.

Again, if you watch a television program like *Law &
Order* or another dramatic serial, you will see obstacle

after obstacle and conflict after conflict heaped on top of each other, each heightening the dramatic tension until, after the climax, resolution is attained. In the aforementioned crime drama, several would-be murder suspects are eliminated from suspicion before settling on an individual who will finally be sitting at the defense table in the courtroom.

As Joseph tells the story of the dream that brought him to Bethlehem, he walks us through the many obstacles he faced on his journey. Joseph's father maligned his dreams from an early age. Mary's unexpected pregnancy filled Joseph with a desire to walk away from their engagement. Joseph questions the reality of his angelic dream. Joseph's friends and family abandon him. On and on, the obstacles and internal and external conflicts pile up, each one providing adequate dramatic tension that draws listeners into the story.

As you craft a first-person narrative sermon you must ask yourself what challenges or obstacles stand in the way of your character fulfilling his or her purpose. If you look at the story and character of Jonah, you can see countless challenges that interrupt God's plan to have Jonah preach to the Ninevites. First, you see Jonah's own obstinacy. Instead of traveling to Nineveh, Jonah goes in the opposite direction. Then, of course, you have the storm, swiftly followed by Jonah being thrown overboard into the raging sea. And while we know that the fish swallows Jonah in order to bring him to Nineveh, Jonah certainly couldn't have known that at the time. Being swallowed by a fish is universally understood as a bad thing! Each one of these events can serve to heighten the dramatic tension of the story, and you must make the most of each of them. What was Jonah thinking when he bought a ticket to Tarshish? How did Jonah feel when the boat was being tossed about by the sea? Was Jonah scared as the great fish opened its mouth to engulf him? In a first-person narrative sermon about Jonah, you would want to take us through each one of these challenges. The greater the obstacle, the more intense the process of resolution. For first-person narrative sermons to captivate your congregation's attention and imagination, you must make the most of the biblical challenges your character had to face.

Working toward Resolution

Human beings desire resolution. When there is conflict, whether it is in a marriage, at work, or in the church, we desire resolution. The tension of people, institutions, or nations at odds with one another is an accepted reality of our lives. Wherever and whenever people rub shoulders with one another, conflict will invariably ensue. However, deep down in the human psyche there is an innate desire for the tension in life to be relieved. We may find ourselves saying, "I don't like conflict," but what we really mean is that our spirit eternally longs for resolution. The best dramatists know that the creation of a story is a carefully constructed dance between conflict and obstacles that help to create tension, as well as avenues and opportunities for resolution that help to ease tension. If you watch or read an effective and engaging drama, you will notice that there are numerous plot twists and turns that serve to continually increase and then release tension. The dramatist will increase and release tension until reaching the moment of climax, upon which the ultimate resolution hinges.

You see this technique used quite effectively in Shakespeare's *Hamlet*. Tension heightens as Hamlet tries to discover if the ghostly message of his father's murder is based in truth. As the "Players" portray a drama for Claudius that mirrors the specific events of the suspected murder, the king flees his stage-side seat in fear and trepidation. The king's guilt is, for Hamlet, evidence that the ghostly apparition spoke the truth. This eases the dramatic tension momentarily. However, the tension is further escalated shortly thereafter, as Hamlet begins to look for an opportunity to kill the king. With each plot twist, the reader's or viewer's attention is arrested, held tightly by their desire to achieve a final resolution.

While resolution is essential, so are the moments of release throughout the drama. Likely, we have all had the experience of watching a movie or reading a book that seemed too heavy. You leave the theater or put the book down, and you feel emotionally exhausted. The exhaustion comes from a lack of release or resolution in the body of the drama. It is true that there are times when dramatists, screenwriters, and novelists intentionally leave a story unresolved, for effect. Some powerful dramas have been crafted this way. I would suggest, however, that your first-person narrative sermons allow for a nice balance of conflict that builds tension and resolution that releases tension. You do not want your people to leave worship feeling as though they have been totally drained.

In the Joseph sermon you can notice numerous emotional peaks and valleys as the sermon works its way to resolution. The disappointment of Joseph's father is countered by Joseph's decision to spend less time with his father. The shame of Mary's unexpected pregnancy is countered by the angelic command of support in Joseph's dream. The demands of a lonely birth are countered by the joy of holding a newborn son. As you construct your first-person narrative sermon, always look for opportunities to use conflict and obstacle to increase dramatic tension, while allowing for a counterbalance of resolution to keep your people interested but not exhausted. If you use dramatic tension effectively, you will find that your congregation will stay with you every step of the way, as you work toward your sermon's ultimate resolution.

Denouement

Agatha Christie was a master at building suspense into her dramatic mysteries. In her play *Ten Little Indians*, ten characters are lured to Indian Island off the coast of England, only to be murdered one after another. As each murder is revealed, the suspicion mounts. Which one of the remaining guests is the villain? Finally, after eight murders, only two characters are left—young Captain Lombard and the beautiful Vera Elizabeth Claythorne. As the climax nears, Ms. Claythorne shoots Captain Lombard, suspecting him to be the murderer. As Captain Lombard falls to the ground, a haunting laugh is heard from offstage. Justice Wargrave, the sixth little Indian supposedly murdered, appears on stage alive and well. Wargrave approaches Vera, ready to extinguish her life. Thus, Wargrave is revealed as the murderer. The remaining moments of the play are called the denouement. The denouement is the resolution of the play that always follows directly after the climax.

Throughout *Ten Little Indians*, the audience has been forced to play a guessing game: who is the murderer? Now, with the mystery solved, all that is left is to tie up any remaining loose ends. In the final moments of the play, with the murderer revealed, final resolution is achieved as the motive for the murders is brought to light. Wargrave makes it clear to Vera that as a judge he had always longed to execute his own justice. Leveling a judgment on a criminal was not nearly as satisfying as executing the sentence itself! Now, at the end of the play, with a noose around Vera's neck, Wargrave has fulfilled his lifelong desire to take the lives of those in whom he finds guilt. Suddenly, a shot rings out. Captain Lombard, who had only been injured by Vera's poor marksmanship, shoots Wargrave to death. Wargrave then falls back onto a couch, dead, and a handful of sentences later the play is over. That is denouement—the swift resolution that immediately follows the climax of a drama.

Your first-person narrative sermon needs a denouement. As I asserted earlier, every sermon you preach should have a point. Preaching is the communication of biblical message to a congregation. I suggest that the denouement is the best place to make your biblical point or message crystal clear. Hopefully, you have taken your people on a narrative journey that has captured both their attention and imagination. You have likely accomplished this by having your character encounter and overcome several conflicts and obstacles, and now, with the dramatic climax behind you, you are free to make your point clear to your people. Notice that in the Joseph sermon, after the climactic birth, the preacher's point is revealed clearly in the denouement.

God is good, that is all I can say. And my father was right. . . . You can be a dreamer, or you can pursue a dream. And God's dreams for your life will always stretch beyond your own wishes, to the well-being of others. Maybe I will never make furniture that will grace the palaces of kings and princes . . . maybe I will only be remembered for this one moment in time. Perhaps I will forever be Joseph, husband of Mary—Mary, the mother of Jesus. That is where my dream has led me . . . and I believe I can live with that. What dream has God laid on your heart? Will you pursue it? It may be the very thing for which you are forever remembered.

The congregation has followed Joseph's journey to Bethlehem, and now, with the birth of Jesus, the resolution, which includes the point of the sermon, is offered to

76

the congregation. If you have been deliberate and careful about the development of your narrative, there is nothing wrong with getting right to the heart of the matter at the denouement. You've told your story, now make your point, and then bring your narrative to an end.

Storyboarding

As I mentioned earlier, you will likely find first-person narrative sermons to be among the easiest messages to remember. Story progression is much easier to recall than typical sermon development. All of us, at one time or another, have told a story. From childhood we have told narratives. "Tell me what you did today at school?" "How did you break your arm?" "How was the prom?" All of these questions are preludes to story. For the preacher who is reluctant to leave the manuscript behind and venture out from the pulpit, delivering a first-person narrative sermon will likely be much less painful and much more enjoyable than he or she might initially anticipate. Nearly everyone can remember and tell a story, and with a bit of training and practice nearly everyone can tell a *good* story.

If, however, a preacher has any trepidation about how to construct and remember a story, it might be helpful to employ the technique of storyboarding. Whether laying out the movement of a television commercial, a television drama, or a feature film, writers, directors, or producers will often lay out a storyboard of their narrative. A storyboard is a scene-by-scene, movement-by-movement, or moment-by-moment pictorial depiction of the narrative. If you go to the "scene selection" queue on any DVD, you will gain a good sense of what a storyboard is.

A storyboard is a frame-by-frame telling of the key movements of a story. If a *Law & Order* episode were to

77

be storyboarded, you might first see a picture of a dead person on a New York City sidewalk, under the caption "The Murder." The next frame would be the officers talking to witnesses, entitled "The Investigation." There would then be a picture of a suspect in handcuffs under the caption "The Arrest." This would be followed by a still of the officers and the suspect in a holding room, entitled "The Interrogation." The storyboard would lay out the entire narrative from beginning to end. Storyboards are helpful for directors and production crews so that they are reminded of the chronology of their work. Storyboards are also helpful to writers as they begin the process of initially laying out their narratives.

When you begin crafting your narrative, try to envision your story in terms of a string of scenes or dramatic moments. Instead of using an outline, try sketching out the progression of your story in pictures. Effective narratives form mental images in the minds of listeners, so why not start by laying out those images on a piece of paper so that they are clear in your mind? If you choose to try storyboarding your first-person narrative sermons, at time of delivery, you will find yourself painting vibrant mental pictures for your congregations, instead of just offering them points or sentences from an outline or manuscript. A storyboard is a dramatic tool that can help you create, organize, and deliver a compelling and well-structured narrative.

6

Writing Character

Writing like People Talk

People do not write like they talk. A term paper for an honors class and a conversation with a neighbor are often radically different discourses—and they should be! One is well-thought-out and orderly, the other is wide-ranging and spontaneous. Many pastors today spend hours in their study crafting a theological paper to be delivered to their congregations on Sunday morning. This type of sermon is dense, with grammatically and theologically correct sentences and ideas. Listening to such a sermon, however, is often a painfully boring experience—the preacher's eyes and head buried in a manuscript the entire time. It feels as if the preacher is talking *at* you, instead of *with* you.

Effective preachers tend to employ a more conversational style of delivery that allows the listeners to feel as though they are part of the conversation. This conversational style is even more important when you are delivering a first-person narrative sermon. When you take on the voice of a biblical character, you are taking on the voice of a flesh-and-blood human being, and interpersonal discourse is always conversational in nature. If you don't learn to write like you talk, or as you envision your character talking, your efforts to communicate character will be futile.

Likewise, to convincingly take on the personality of a biblical character, you absolutely cannot read or even glance at a manuscript. With other types of sermon delivery, the use of a manuscript or notes may be entirely acceptable. Audiences are accustomed to listening to tremendously accomplished orators who use notes, manuscripts, and teleprompters to aid them in their delivery of a message. However, when you enter into a conversation with someone, you never bring notes or a manuscript! When you are telling a story to your friends, you don't write it down and read it to them—you speak directly to them. You establish eye contact. You make a connection. A manuscript inserted into the conversation would be an abnormal barrier to communication.

You are bound to fail in delivering an effective first-person narrative sermon if you are using a manuscript or notes. In first-person narratives, you are trying to speak through a biblical character—and real people just don't begin a conversation by opening a notebook and reading. To deliver an effective first-person narrative, not only do you have to step away from your manuscript, but, when preparing your message, you need to learn how to write the way people speak.

Listening to People

You may have noticed that the way people speak is quite different from how they would write. When a

80

person has time to write down their thoughts, they can organize, edit, and refine their discourse. They may begin with a rough draft, but their goal is a polished masterpiece. Conversation with a friend is always a rough draft. Listen to the way people talk. When we converse with one another, we do not speak in grammatically correct sentences. We pause. We stutter. We become distracted. We lose our train of thought. We repeat words and sentences for emphasis. We use slang. We go off on tangents. We beat around the bush. We hem and haw until we get to the point. We dance around difficult issues. Sometimes our words race out of our mouths unchecked, while at other times our silence speaks louder than our words.

When you begin to craft a first-person narrative, you need to begin by writing the way you believe your character would have actually spoken. I believe you should always fully write out a sermon before you begin to work on its delivery. While it is important not to rely on a manuscript when delivering your sermon, drafting your message in manuscript form can be essential in helping you focus your story line and character development.

If you look at truly fine dramatic work, you will notice that accomplished dramatists have mastered the ability to write as people talk. The following monologue is from the Pulitzer Prize–winning play *Wit* by Margaret Edson. Vivian is a highly regarded literary scholar and professor. Vivian cares deeply about proper diction and the sonnets of John Donne, and is aggressively battling terminal ovarian cancer. Toward the end of the play, pain and loss begin to erode Vivian's razor-sharp wit and will to live. She has been a willing participant in an experimental trial for a new type of cancer treatment. The treatment has failed.

In this particular scene, Vivian has just received a popsicle from her nurse, Susie. Popsicles are just about the only thing Vivian can eat at this point. Susie talks to

Vivian about her "code status"—what Vivian wants the doctors to do if her heart stops beating. Vivian opts for a DNR—a Do Not Resuscitate order. Just as Susie is about to leave the room, Vivian asks Susie if she will continue to take care of her. Susie responds, "'Course, sweetheart. Don't you worry." In the following monologue, notice how the writing reflects the speaking patterns of a real person in real pain. Take note of the pauses, the interrupted thought, and the natural flow of the conversation Vivian is directly having with the audience. There is no question that Vivian is speaking like a real live human being . . . who is, of course, dying.

That certainly was a *maudlin* display. Popsicles? "Sweetheart?" I can't believe my life has become so . . . *corny*. But it can't be helped. I don't see any other way. We are discussing life and death, and not in the abstract either; we are discussing *my* life and *my* death, and my brain is dulling, and poor Susie's was never that sharp to begin with, and I can't conceive of any other . . . *tone*. Now is not the time for verbal swordplay, for unlikely flights of imagination and wildly shifting perspective, for metaphysical conceit, for wit. And nothing would be worse than a detailed scholarly analysis. Erudition. Interpretation. Complication. Now is a time for simplicity. Now is a time for, dare I say, kindness.

I thought being extremely smart would take care of it. Ooohhh. I'm scared. Oh, God. I want . . . I want . . . No. I want to hide. I just want to curl up in a little ball. I want to tell you how it feels. I want to explain it, to use *my* words. It's as if . . . I can't . . . There aren't . . . I am like a student and this is the final exam and I don't know what to put down because I don't understand the question and I'm *running out of time*. The time for extreme measures has come. I'm in terrible pain. Susie says that I need to begin aggressive pain management if I am going to stand it. "It": such a little word. In this case, I think "it" signifies "being alive." I apologize in advance for what this palliative treatment modality does to the dramatic coherence of my play's last scene. It can't be helped. They have to do something. I'm in terrible pain. Say it, Vivian. *It hurts like hell. It really does.* Oh, God. Oh, God.

This monologue is helpful for many reasons, as we reflect on how we write the way people talk. Note the one-word sentences. So often in discourse, we respond with a single word. The pauses are particularly effective because they are so real. When have you ever heard someone speak nonstop without pausing to either take a breath, consider a thought, or regain composure? And the pauses are clearly active space. Thoughts are changing, and direction is shifting throughout these momentary breaks. In this monologue, there are times when Vivian addresses the audience directly, and then there are moments when she is addressing herself. Conversation is always active, even when it is being shared from a hospital bed. When our sermons contain dramatic monologue or dialogue, we should be keenly aware of crafting our words just as someone would speak them in conversation. If you can learn to write your first-person narrative like someone would actually speak, you will be well on your way to creating a truly believable dramatic experience for your congregation.

Eavesdropping

The first step toward being able to write as people speak is to take time to listen to people as they talk. Eavesdrop. When you go out, whether it is to a coffee shop, a grocery store, or your child's dance recital, listen to the way people communicate with one another. Do they ramble on about nothing? Are they direct? Do they use any catchphrases? Are they loud? Do they whisper?

83

Do they look at the person they are addressing, or are they checking out someone else while trying to hold a conversation? Do they grunt? Do they say "umm, umm" when trying to convey a thought? I believe it is essential for a preacher to always carry along a small notepad to jot down illustrations and observations. If you intend to become an effective first-person narrative preacher, take notes on the people you overhear speaking. How do people transition from one topic of conversation to another? What happens when someone loses their train of thought? How do they recover? Make notes because you may encounter a turn of phrase or a manner of conversing that you might want to adopt or adapt for a first-person narrative. Countless dramatists make a habit of going out and listening to the way people speak. The best dramatists can write dialogue and monologue that incorporates the inconsistent pacing, the abrupt transitions, and the intermittent focus of real conversation.

Listening to Biblical Conversation

We need to be listening to biblical dialogue and monologue as well. If your scripture passage has your character actually speaking, those words should make their way right into your sermon. Biblical dialogue or monologue is an absolute gift when crafting a first-person narrative sermon! If you are taking on the role of Mary at the time of Gabriel's announcement that she will bear a child, your sermon will have to include, "Here am I, the servant of the Lord; let it be with me according to your word" (Luke 1:38). Biblical dialogue should always be included in your first-person narratives. If the Bible says your character made a specific statement, then you should use it in your sermon. In fact, that statement can often help you get an understanding of how your character might have actually spoken. The use of biblical dialogue in your sermon is also an important educational tool. Remember, the more Bible we get into our sermons, the more Bible will get into our people!

Verbal Object of Intensity

When you are speaking with someone, do you look intently into their eyes? Are you entirely focused on the person you are talking to? Or does your focus wander a bit? The next conversation you have, notice what you are doing during the experience. You will likely be surprised how little you focus on the other person. You will be talking and picking lint off your sweater. You will be speaking directly to someone, and yet you will be pouring yourself a drink. You will be in the midst of a heated debate while examining the length of your fingernails. The only times we ever truly look directly into someone's eyes and speak to them is when we have something crucially important to say, and we feel it is crucially important to be heard.

Professional actors often learn the art of using "object of intensity" when they are engaged in dialogue. An "object of intensity" is something—anything—an actual person might be doing while talking with someone. An effective object of intensity will help facilitate more natural dialogue. Take a novice actor and give them a monologue to perform, and they may deliver that entire monologue directly to their audience with perfect focus and concentration. The problem is that conversations never happen that way. We rarely, if ever, give our full attention to a conversation when we are in it. The actor's monologue will come off stiff and unnatural.

If, however, you have that same actor deliver their monologue while setting the table for dinner, you will

85

see a remarkable transformation. The actor has to focus on the table settings; the forks, knives, plates, glasses, and napkins become objects of intensity that help to distract the actor's focus. As a result, there are suddenly natural pauses, less frequent eye contact with the audience, and distractions that allow for a more natural discourse. Pouring a drink, polishing a table, knitting, biting nails, taking off shoes—all can serve as effective objects of intensity that will help a dramatic monologue flow more naturally. Objects of intensity help performers speak as people naturally speak.

Now, please understand, I am not suggesting that you knit during your next first-person narrative sermon. While it would likely help the flow of your spoken word, it is important to remember that we are preachers, not actors. We are called primarily to praise, not to perform. With that said, our performance should be as solid as possible. Personally, I discourage the use of props and costumes when delivering a first-person narrative sermon. I do not believe worship should resemble your local community theater, with tired costumes and questionable prop choices.

So, how can a preacher get the benefit of having an object of intensity without bringing yarn and needles into the chancel area? There is a way to construct a written or verbal object of intensity that can be just as helpful. In the Joseph sermon in the previous chapter, there is a good example of this. Joseph is talking about making a chair:

> I spent more time with my friends and dabbling in the building of chairs. I would carve the backrests and armrests—inlaying symbols and images with olive wood into the seats. It could take me weeks to finish a single piece.

What does this brief statement have to do with anything? Arguably nothing. However, the chair that is

86

envisioned by Joseph in that very moment is an effective object of intensity. Joseph can see the chair in front of him. He can trace the carvings with his finger. He can touch the olive inlays with his hand. He can admire the chair for a brief moment. The chair is not physically there, of course; Joseph merely sees it in his mind. In that moment, the preacher's focus is effectively distracted from the congregation, and his discourse flows all the more naturally. Similarly, Mary and the baby Jesus often serve as Joseph's object of intensity in this sermon.

> And Mary has been extraordinary. We had to travel ninety miles from Nazareth to Bethlehem. Mary didn't complain once. Over a week we trekked over mountain ridges and through valleys . . . I would look at Mary and . . . well, she seemed to me more like an angel than a woman. I saw the strength of God in her. And tonight. Here in Bethlehem. In my hometown. With every door closed to us—all alone—Mary gave birth in a barn. She encouraged me more than I encouraged her. We wrapped the child in cloths. I gave him his name. Jesus. And then we laid him in a cattle trough so Mary could rest.

Joseph gets lost in his image of Mary and his son. Mary on the donkey. The journey itself. The mountain ridges and valleys. The town of Bethlehem around him. Holding Jesus. Laying Jesus in a manger. Each one of these images offers opportunities for distracted thought. Distractions, pauses, moments of reflection are incredibly helpful when you are writing character. Distractions, interruptions, and momentary silences are a natural part of every conversation. They help facilitate the relaxed flow of discourse, and they are effective windows through which the congregation can catch a glimpse of what is most important to your character.

Tangents and Throwaway Lines

"Don't go off on a tangent," we say when we want someone to focus. The length of all church meetings could be greatly reduced if tangents were avoided. But people go off on tangents when they are speaking, and so should your character. Granted, you have only a handful of minutes to convey a biblical concept to your congregation, but you may want to take a moment to go off on a brief tangent. Like an object of intensity, tangents and throw-away lines do not necessarily further the plotline of your story, but they are effective devices in revealing character. When Joseph was talking about his engagement to Mary, the whole scene could have been greatly enhanced if he had taken a moment to reminisce about their "first date." Tracing back a simple wisp of a memory could have told us so much about Joseph. How did Joseph first meet Mary? What was his first impression of her? Was Joseph pleased with his parents' selection of a bride? Was he nervous? Would any of that have helped further the homiletical point that God grants us dreams that are meant to be pursued for the benefit of others as much as for ourselves? Directly, no. Indirectly, you bet!

The more the congregation can relate to Joseph, the more likely they are to take seriously the questions he asks them at the end of the message: "What dream has God laid on your heart? Will you pursue it? It may be the very thing for which you are forever remembered." Don't forget, we want our friends, our role models, and our politicians to be "real." The more authentic someone appears, the more likely we are to follow their lead. The same holds true for the characters you present to your congregation.

Throwaway lines are sentences that are not of crucial importance to communicate. These are the words you

88

speak under your breath, the ones that if people don't hear them, it doesn't really matter. Someone says, "What was that?" "Oh, nothing. Not important." And yet, because throwaway lines are part of natural discourse, they are important. Effective communication is more than just an arrangement of articulate and perfectly audible sentences. When Joseph shares his initial responses to Mary's pregnancy, his voice trails off.

> I was beside myself—I was furious. I remember I said things . . . I called her things . . . I was *certain* . . . she had betrayed me. Mary was pregnant, and I was not the father. How could she do this to me? Did she have any idea what people would say? I would have to live with this humiliation for the rest of my life.

None of these sentences are particularly important in and of themselves. There isn't a single line that needs to be delivered with particular intensity. Joseph's fury and regret is what is important to convey. It is entirely appropriate for Joseph's voice to trail off. In fact, you are the author, so you are free to drop a line mid-sentence. If Joseph had merely said, "I remember I said things, called her things . . . I was *certain* . . . How could she do this to me?" we still would have gotten the point. Don't be afraid of throwing away lines that are meant to convey a feeling more than a point. The more natural you are, the more believable your character will be, and the more likely the congregation will receive the point you are trying to make.

Focus Point

Objects of intensity, tangents, and throwaway lines also allow you to set a congregation up. Your intentional lack of focus, at times, will allow your intentional focus to be particularly riveting. If your character is intensely focused from start to finish on your sermon, you will weary your congregation, and when it is time to make your point, you will have no way of heightening their focus. There is real power in being able to suddenly look intently at your congregation and deliver a particularly important line. And there will likely be a number of times when you want your congregation to hear and *get* exactly what it is you are saying.

This happens several times during the Joseph sermon. It happens when Joseph relates the words of his father, "Boys dream, Joseph; men pursue dreams. And the only dreams worth pursuing—the only dreams that are from God—are ones that benefit others as much as yourself." The congregation has to be set up to hear that critically important line. Joseph needs to bring particular focus to that moment in order to make the point. Likewise, Joseph needs to be able to heighten intensity for the delivery of those final lines, "What dream has God laid on your heart? Will you pursue it? It may be the very thing for which you are forever remembered." Often in first-person narrative sermons you will make your point with only a sentence or two. You want to write your character and story in such a way that when you are ready to deliver your homiletical idea, your congregation is glued to your every word.

7

Getting into Character

Beyond the Written Word

For the preacher of a first-person narrative sermon, designing a character, crafting a dramatic monologue, and writing as people speak is the halfway point. You have created the character; now it is time to *get into* the character. While the act of worship should always be an act of praise more than an act of performance, to be believable and effective, a first-person narrative sermon needs to be performance-quality. This sermon style requires that you shed your own personality and take on the persona of another. If Pastor Jim is playing the role of Abraham, Abraham should not simply resemble Pastor Jim in a robe holding a staff. Once the dramatic monologue has been written, the body and voice work has to begin. For your character to be believable, your congregation has to slowly forget about you and start seeing your character come to life through your body and voice.

Again, if you are taking on the character of Abraham, you must begin to ask questions about Abraham. How would Abraham walk? How would he move? At age ninety, how would Abraham hold his body? What would his physical limitations be? If you are a twenty-five-year-old pastor portraying the aged Abraham, you shouldn't bound around the chancel of your church as you otherwise might on a typical Sunday morning. The questions continue. How would Abraham speak? Would his speech be rapid with youthful enthusiasm, or would it be more considered and slower? As Abraham speaks, would his thoughts be clear, or would there be moments when he loses his train of thought?

As was true when you began preparing your dramatic monologue, as you begin to get into character, the more questions you can ask and answer about your character, the more successful you will be in your delivery. When an actor receives a script and a role to play, getting into that character becomes their primary responsibility. They ask countless questions—questions of the text, questions about the era the character lived in, questions about the relationships the character maintains. In theater, unlike film and television, the playwright is rarely available to answer the actor's questions. Shakespeare cannot be consulted when an actor is trying to understand the particular motivations behind Hamlet's actions. As a first-person narrative preacher, you are at a decided advantage. You are the writer, director, and actor. You already know the motivations behind all of your character's actions and words, and if you don't, you should. Getting into character should be relatively easy, because you, and you alone, have already outlined the character, the plot, and every word of the monologue.

The downside of being solely responsible for the dramatic integrity of your piece from its creation to its performance is that you are not an unbiased observer. You are invested in every aspect of the production. You become inherently uncritical. There are reasons why plays, films, and television shows have separate actors, directors, writers, and producers. Each role requires a certain competency, and the dramatic collaboration serves as a system of checks and balances that can help to ensure a quality performance. While the use of video recordings can help any preacher evaluate his or her work in any sermon style, it can be essential to the development of a first-person narrative preacher. When you witness yourself perform, you can see whether *your* personality has been revealed or the personality of *the character* you are trying to portray. Video recording can offer you answers to important questions. Do you sound like you are preaching, or do you sound like you are having a natural conversation? Are some of your trademark mannerisms present in your character, or have you been able to adjust your movement so that a different physical character is being represented? The goal of getting into character can be summed up in the words John the Baptist used in regard to Jesus in the Gospel of John: *"He must increase, I must decrease."* Using video recordings to critique your performance can tell you who has increased—does your congregation see more of you or more of your character? As you become more proficient at getting into character, the visibility of your character will increase, while the visibility of your personality will decrease.

The Instrument

Any character you choose to portray will be revealed through your body. As every actor knows, when performing a dramatic monologue *you* are the primary instrument. This is true of preachers as well. Your body is an instrument. Therefore, it seems important to say a word or two about taking care of your instrument.

If an instrument is essential to a performance, it needs to be tended to diligently. The next time you attend the symphony, have no doubt that the concert master's Stradivarius is in perfect condition. When you board a plane, you may find yourself praying that the mechanics' tools have all been perfectly calibrated and maintained. If you are a sports fan, you expect that your team has been keeping in shape in the off-season so that they can perform on opening day. As a preacher, as a deliverer of first-person narrative sermons, you must take equal care of your instrument. Caring for your body should be a priority for you. If you step to your pulpit overweight and out of shape, it is like showing up to the concert hall with a rusted trumpet, or to the speedway with a flat tire, or to the basketball court with a sprained ankle; you will either be unable to perform or embarrassed in doing so. Too many pastors take dreadfully poor care of themselves. Instead of treating our instruments like temples in which God's Holy Spirit dwells, we treat them like garbage cans, filling them with all kinds of refuse and emptying them when we remember. The care of a preacher's instrument should be of primary importance.

We should regulate our diets. Soda, fried foods, fist-fuls of candy, decadent desserts, and heaping helpings should not be a part of our lives. Our diets should be balanced, healthy, and modest. We should eat to live, not live to eat!

And we must exercise regularly. It has been suggested that those of us who spend much of our time in cars, behind desks, and sitting in meetings should find crea-tive ways to get in a bit of exercise each day. Walk to lunch. Take the stairs instead of the elevator. Speed walk around the office before work. As preachers we must get to the gym. We must work out aerobically and anaerobically. Three to five times a week, we should work up a sweat. We must build the strength of our instrument. Run on the treadmill, use the elliptical machines, work out with weights, swim, play basketball, play tennis, take a spinning class, do water aerobics—don't just get active, get fit!

As you commit to being fit, you must also strive to be flexible. You should make time every day to stretch out your instrument. A few moments in the beginning and end of your day to stretch out your back, your legs, your arms, your neck, can help you stay healthy, physically engaged, and injury-free. Taking time to stretch and sense your body can also help detect bodily abnormalities that should be checked out by a physician.

Making regular visits to your doctor for annual check-ups is crucially important, too. And as inconvenient as they may be, routine tests such as colonoscopies, stress tests, mammograms, and prostate screens are essential in maintaining the health of your primary instrument. As Christians, we believe in life everlasting. We believe our earthly bodies will one day be replaced with heavenly bodies. So, please understand that these efforts are not a vain attempt to add years to your life; they are an attempt to add life to your years, and energy and vitality to your vocation. Don't just prepare to preach on Sunday, prepare to preach for the rest of your life!

Voice

Your voice is the primary means of communicating your sermon. Whatever sermon style you choose to employ in a given week, fluctuations in your volume and verbal pacing will help you to engage your audience.

When attempting to communicate a character, you need to pay even closer attention to your vocal options. Sometimes a character will whisper. Sometimes they will shout. Sometimes their voice will tremble with emotion. Sometimes their voice will trail off in despair or sorrow. Sometimes a character will talk rapidly with great excitement, while at other times silence will speak louder than words. The great vocal challenge in any dramatic performance is that the actor, or in our case, the preacher, has to deliver sentences and thoughts as if this is the first time he or she has ever thought of them.

We have all been cautioned at one time or another to think before we speak. That caution is in response to the reality that we are often speaking while we are thinking. Too often, we think out loud. As a result, most of our natural discourse is not particularly considered or premeditated. That is why, minutes after a heated exchange, when the other person has left, we think of what we *should* have said to them. When delivering a first-person narrative sermon, you need to create the impression that your character is speaking their thoughts as they come to mind.

In a normal sermon, the congregation expects that you have done all your work and have considered every point and idea you share with them. They expect that what you present them is well-thought-out and orderly. In a first-person narrative sermon, it is ideal if you can create a sense that the character has not fully thought out what he or she is about to say. There are many ways to create this appearance while knowing exactly where you are going in your sermon. Again, appropriate modulation of your volume and pacing is essential as you share your dramatic monologue.

A wonderful pacing technique is the use of silence. Pay attention to the next conversation you have. Take note of how many times you pause while talking. You may pause to consider a thought. You may pause to choose your next word. You may pause because you are overcome with emotion. You may pause because an image has come to mind and you want to mentally take it in. If you pay attention to your own natural discourse, you will be amazed by the amount of silence that is present. It is active silence to be sure, but it is silence all the same. The technique of searching for a word can be particularly helpful in facilitating a sense of natural discourse. Think of how many times a word or phrase has been on the tip of your tongue and it has taken a second or two to get it out. It happens to all of us. Take any sentence you speak: *"Tuesday my wife and I went to Jordan's Furniture to buy a beige ottoman to match our family room sofa."* That is a very cleanly conveyed thought. However, we seldom speak as cleanly as that. A more natural statement might be: *"What day was it? Wednesday? No. Tuesday. Tuesday my wife and I went to Jordan's Furniture to buy a beige ottoman to match our family room sofa."* Or, *"Tuesday my wife and I went to . . . what's that big store on Route 9 in Natick? It's got the big purple neon sign . . . Jordan's—Jordan's Furniture. We went there to buy a beige ottoman to match our family room sofa."* Or, an extreme example, *"Monday—Tuesday. Tuesday my wife and I went to . . . that furniture store . . . you know . . . the big one on Route 9. We bought this tan-ish . . . beige . . . oh, what do you call it? The thing that you put your feet on—an ottoman! We went to buy this beige ottoman to match our family room sofa."* Pausing, searching for words, and repeating information when you get it right are all components of natural discourse. While you don't want to overuse these vocal techniques, they are central to the art of speaking written words as if they have come into your character's mind for the very first time.

Movement

Movement is crucially important when trying to establish character. As I mentioned earlier, you want to consider how your particular character would move. It is also important to be keenly aware of how *you* move. A first-person narrative sermon naturally lends itself to extraneous or nervous movement. Without a manuscript or notes to ground a preacher, nervous energy can be quite acute. If a pastor has a natural tendency to pace, that tendency will be further accentuated in a first-person narrative sermon. When you are in character, all your movements need to be motivated. You don't move side to side, you don't bounce on your toes, you don't pace back and forth, because people rarely do that when they are having a conversation. If you move, it is because your character has a purpose in moving. And movement always precedes the spoken word. If your character wants to take note of Mount Tabor in the distance, they will move in the direction of Tabor and perhaps even motion to it before they mention it. If your character is describing an argument they had with someone in which they shook their finger at the other person in anger, as they tell the story, they would shake their finger just before they mention it. They would begin to shake their finger and then say, *"I shook my finger at him and told him the next time he had something to say about me, he'd better say it to my face."* In the Joseph sermon, the preacher, when describing the chairs Joseph would make, would first move toward and motion to the imagined chairs just before he described them. Gestures, posture, facial expressions, and directional movement will speak volumes about your character. Make sure your movement is natural and justifiable for your character, and you will find that your character is all the more convincing to your congregation. Again, making good use of video recording can help you with this kind of analysis.

Costumes and Props

As I have already indicated, I am not a fan of preachers using props, costumes, or sets during first-person narrative sermons. It is true that you will rarely, if ever, see a dramatic performance that doesn't employ props, costumes, and sets. However, in productions that utilize these theatrical devices, you will find that costume designers, set designers, and prop managers are employed to ensure that all three are of the highest quality and are effectively used. When members of your congregation go to a theatrical production, they usually experience a product that has been thoroughly researched, designed, and supported by professionals. As preachers, we will never have the time, money, talent, or eye for the professional costuming our parishioners are accustomed to, from the performances they attend and the movies and television shows they watch. At best, our costume and prop usage can look like the children's Christmas pageant gone terribly wrong. At worst, our efforts can serve to distract our congregants from the message we are trying to communicate.

Costumes and props hold tremendous visual power over audiences. It is an often quoted rule that you never place a gun on stage in the first act if you don't plan on using it by the third act. If you are going to bring a prop on stage, you'd better plan to make good use of it, otherwise your audience will spend much of their time wondering what it will be used for, and they will lose much of the sermon. Undoubtedly, you have been to a dramatic performance where a piece of someone's costume has come undone. A character's scarf falls to the ground as the character storms out of the room. You will notice that one of the actors who remains on the stage will pick up the scarf as naturally as possible and take it offstage with them when they exit. You see, directors know that as soon as the scarf falls to the ground, the audience's focus is almost exclusively on the scarf until it is picked up. It could be the most riveting moment of the play, yet the audience is wondering, *Is anyone going to pick up that scarf? What if someone slips on or gets tangled up in the scarf? Did anyone notice the scarf fall to the ground?* The play suddenly is about a scarf lying on the floor, rather than the drama the artists were attempting to convey.

Likewise, you will never see a significant piece of furniture positioned "down center" on a stage. The most powerful spot on any stage is down center. Down center is dead center in front of the first row of the audience. Down center is always where the most critical dramatic action in the play occurs. You would never put a table or a chair or a desk down center, because that automatically makes the play about a table or a chair or a desk.

Costumes, props, and sets hold tremendous power over the audience; if you misuse them you will lose your audience. If your Abraham is dressed in a shepherd's costume from last year's Christmas pageant, your first-person narrative will be about the shepherd's costume. If Abraham enters the sanctuary wearing sunglasses and talking on a cell phone, the dramatic monologue will be about the sunglasses and the cell phone. Our goal in every sermon is to help focus people on the Word of God; don't distract them from God's Word with a poor attempt at a costume or the awkward use of a prop. As a rule of thumb, never use any costume, prop, or set that doesn't substantially further the point you are trying to make in your sermon. It might be humorous or cute to see the beloved pastor dressed as David with his stone and sling in hand, but that reaction will be short-lived. Don't give your people costumes and props—give them the unobstructed and powerful Word of God.

To Read or Not to Read

It is a dilemma every preacher faces at one time or another. Should a preacher use a manuscript? Should he or she preach from notes or an outline? Should a sermon be extemporaneous? Is it best to memorize your sermon? How important is a conversational style? There is no shortage of opinions on how sermons should be delivered. I have always believed that preachers should employ whatever style allows them to most freely connect with their congregation. If a preacher is so tied to a manuscript that there isn't even occasional eye contact with the parishioners, if a preacher is so worried about losing the train of thought during an extemporaneous sermon that he or she regularly loses the train of thought, if a memorized sermon sounds stiff, rigid, and unnatural, that preacher needs to employ a different delivery style. Don't choose a style based on what is most comfortable to you. Rather, choose a delivery style that allows you to communicate most effectively with your people. Some preachers can use a manuscript to great effect, while others find that a skeletal outline works best for them. There should be no sacred cows when it comes to sermon delivery. You simply need to do what works best for you and for your congregation.

First-person narrative sermons are a clear exception. When you take on a particular character, when you play a role, when you act a part, you simply cannot read. Outlines, notes, and manuscripts have no place in first-person narrative sermons. The second you glance at a piece of paper, you have fallen out of character. Unless you are playing a character that is delivering a speech, you should never read. People don't enter into personal conversations with a manuscript in hand. None of the biblical characters you will portray would have written out their remarks before speaking them. You will never find an actor in a play, film, or television production reading from a script. Scripts are fine for rehearsal, but scripts are never acceptable on stage. You can choose to memorize your first-person narrative, you can choose to deliver your sermon extemporaneously, or you can do a combination of both. The goal is to get into character. Clinging to a manuscript, reading your first-person narrative, is totally out of character. Don't do it—ever!

The good news is that most preachers who deliver a first-person narrative sermon find such sermons to be particularly easy to remember. This kind of sermon has a distinct story line, and story lines are so much easier to remember than traditional sermon points and transitions. And the wonderful thing about dramatic monologues is that if you lose your train of thought, you can be confident that characters do that, and often. Some of the best and most natural moments in live theater occur when one character loses his or her place. When you are truly in character, you can make split-second decisions in character. If you stay in character, and if you have taken the time to really *know* your character, when you lose your place you will naturally make choices that your character would make. In this particular sermon style, you can make a mistake and no one will ever know the difference. The only real mistake you can ever make is dropping your character. If you get off track, if you miss a key line, or if you lose your place, don't ever allow it to register on your character's face. Get in character, stay in character, and you will effectively convey your character to your people.

8

Pastor vs. Playwright

An Experiment

I have been trying to make a case for pastors to approach first-person narrative sermons as if they were dramatic monologues because of the wealth of theatrical resources available to help them craft these messages. I contend that a critical study of dramatic writing and performance can greatly enhance the overall effectiveness of first-person narrative sermons. Simply put, if pastors had some instruction in crafts like playwriting and screenwriting, their characters and the stories they tell would be far richer and much more engaging. In an attempt to further build my case, I asked both a gifted preacher and a gifted playwright to attempt to write a first-person narrative sermon. While both individuals were highly proficient in their respective vocations, neither had ever crafted a first-person narrative sermon. I gave the pastor and the playwright exactly the same scripture and the same instructions. There were to use the story of the prodigal son as their story line. They could choose to portray any character in the story they wanted to, but they had to try to get across the message that God welcomes people back *as they are*, with unconditional love.

With no formal training and limited instruction, the Reverend Jim Conley and Leslie Dillen approached their assignment with enthusiasm and good humor. I insisted that I receive their first drafts. I wanted their initial impulses and instincts. I didn't want their most polished and professional work. I wanted to see their first responses to the task. Pastors, unlike playwrights, don't have the luxury of writing and rewriting their sermon countless times before it is performed. So often a sermon's first draft is its only draft. Both Jim and Leslie have graciously offered their first drafts for this exercise, I have no doubt their efforts would be even more impressive if they had been given additional time to reshape and revise their initial work.

Having witnessed many first-person narrative sermons, and even more dramatic monologues, I had good reason to suspect that the pastor and the playwright would differ in their individual strengths. I suspected that the pastor would be more effective than the playwright in communicating the core message of the text because of playwrights' natural aversion to being preachy. At the same time, I expected much more artistry in the discourse composed by the playwright because of playwrights' constant attempt to make dialogue and monologue "real." Because both Jim and Leslie are gifted communicators, I was confident that their work would help to shed light on how the study of dramatic monologue can enhance the creation of first-person narrative sermons. As you read the following sermons, take note of their respective strengths and weaknesses. What dramatic decisions help to bring the characters alive, and what decisions prove to be problematic? Are there dramatic moments that would be difficult to translate to a congregation on a Sunday morning? What, if anything, can a pastor learn about dramatic monologue from a playwright?

The Playwright

More than Meets the Eye
by Leslie Dillen

You tell me what I'm supposed to do here? And don't tell me "There's more to that boy than meets the eye." Don't I know it now? All that boy's put us through—a hell of a lot more than meets the eye. I'm sorry Becky, I'm sorry. I know I shouldn't swear, I shouldn't be angry but I am, I am. Who does he think he is coming back into our lives like this? I tell you there are times I've been grateful, grateful you were dead and didn't have to go through what Keith's put us through. "At least your Mother's not alive to hear about this," I told him. Not that it made any difference. It just gave him an excuse to stop writing or calling and keep doing whatever he was doing to further himself in "La La land" as he calls it. "La La land"! Can you imagine a grown man talking like that?

You wouldn't know him now Becky, you wouldn't know him. He got selfish, mean. Everything is about getting ahead, getting the money, getting the parts, getting famous—nothing about his family, nothing about us. Oh no. We don't fit into his world anymore. When Johnny came up with that invention for inseminating the cattle, Keith could have cared less. I don't think we'd be doing so well now if Johnny hadn't thought up that machine. "Ranching has to change from butchering to birthing," Johnny said. That was great. You'd be so proud of him. But Keith couldn't be bothered to give his brother five minutes of credit. And you know Johnny he doesn't ask

105

for much. You know that. He has a plan, follows through, and gets the job done. Like me. But Keith.

He's your son, looks more like you than Johnny does. I guess that's the way these things work. We favor the child most like us, but that doesn't seem right somehow. I really tried not to be that way with Keith. It made me proud how people always liked Keith, right off. No matter if he didn't do anything much or say anything. Just like you, he could walk in a room and people would want to be with him, talk with him. But the thing is, he knew it. I could see he did. It made me mad sometimes Becky. It gave him an air of pride I didn't like. When he came to tell me he wanted to go to LA and be an actor I didn't want him to do it. And then when he asked for his share of the money you left him, it was all I could do not to get out my belt. That attitude of entitlement and why shouldn't he have it now. Why should he? Who does he think he is that he can just leave everything and go do what he wants? There are obligations in life a person has to fulfill and why shouldn't he have to fulfill his?

But then I see your eyes Becky, your eyes in our son, looking back at me. I can hear your voice in my heart saying, "There's more to that boy than meets the eye. Let him find out what that is. Let him go." I know you're right. Don't we all want a chance to find out what we can do with our lives?

But we don't all get that chance Becky. We don't all get that chance. When my daddy told me I'd better like ranching cause that's all I was good for, I wanted to show him he was wrong. I wanted to leave right then, go off, make myself into a new self. But I was in love with you. I wanted to make you proud, make you a home, make a family with you. How could I leave? I don't mean to say it's your fault.

Okay. Maybe I do. Sometimes I wish I'd never had a family, just gone off like Keith—to hell with everybody else—and do what I want to do, whatever that would have been. Forgive me Becky. Well no use looking back is there? I could see all that possibility, that hope that

106

excitement in Keith's eyes and I say, "Okay, but you've got to understand this is all there is. The rest will go to your brother." "Fine by me." And he's gone, just like that.

We missed him, but Johnny and me have been used to doing things ourselves anyway. Sometimes I wonder if Johnny's upset or wishes he'd gone. I asked him one day if he wanted to go, if he wanted to do something else. "No," he says, "ranching is what I love." He's already looking at where he wants to build his home on the property. I tell him, insisting like, he could go if he wants to but no he says he's just fine where he is. He's thrived since Keith left. He really has. I'd hate to see that go backwards. I know it shouldn't make any difference if Keith were back, but it would, you know it would. He's always got to be the center of attention. And is that gonna change because he's had some hard times, had some hard knocks? I don't think so.

You know what I think? I think, good, come back home with your tail between your legs—proves you're not so special after all. God help me, what makes us want to hurt others when we've been hurt? I'm not proud of the way I feel Becky, but there it is. What am I supposed to do?

Why can't I believe like you did that there's more to that boy than meets the eye? All I see is a boy who's wasted his life and broke our hearts. Yeah, right. Who am I to judge? Would I have done it any differently? Would I have done it better? Maybe not.

I have dreams about Keith. Did you send them Becky? I keep trying to find him. I can hear him talking in another room or calling for help but I can't get to him. The doors won't open or the room's empty when I get there.

Johnny and I don't talk about Keith much. We talk about you some and how we miss your laughing or teasing us, or some silly memory like when that horse threw you and you kicked it. But not Keith, till the other day when Johnny found an old box in the barn full of stuff Keith had collected—bird feathers, rocks, a chipmunk skull. We just looked at the pieces for a while. "Wonder what he was going to do with these?" That's all Johnny said. Then he closes the box up and is about to throw it away, but I stop him and I put it back on the shelf. Like that time I found your hairbrush in the bottom of the drawer and put it back like you might come back to reclaim it. Did I think Keith would come back? Did I hope he might? I was afraid he was joining you in death and my heart was closing up to you both.

After that I'd find myself repeating, there's more to that boy than meets the eye, like a chant or a prayer to keep him safe and to keep him alive somehow. I don't know how to pray like you did. I certainly don't know God like you did. I don't know what to do. I don't know how to open my heart and let this boy come back home. I don't have it in me. I don't. I don't know what to do except fall down on this floor and wish to God you were here to help me.

Wait. Didn't Keith say that? What was it? He said it once right after you died? Something about the floor, the falling down . . . wait what was it? Falling down faith. That's it. Yes that's it. Right after you died, I got drunk and was crying on the kitchen floor. Keith found me and asked, "What are you doing down there?" "Trying to find my faith," I said. "Looks to me like you found falling down faith." Made me laugh. "What kind of faith is that?" I asked him. He says, "That's the kind of faith you need when life knocks the wind out of you and you don't know if you can stand up and breathe again."

Keith said that. He said that. How could I have forgotten that?

That's what I need right now when I feel his presence come to me over the Green Horn Mountains, moving through the pastures of rye, past the antelope looking through the snow fences at the highway, coming up our dirt road. Slow steps. Hesitant. Walking a road he'd grown up on as though he is a stranger in a foreign land. I will run. Some of the men will look at me like I've lost my mind. Never walk when I can ride. "Its Keith," I'll call back, "Keith is coming home."

Oh Becky, he's aged ten years, tired, thin. He was surprised when I grabbed him and hugged him tight. You were always the one who hugged.

Johnny doesn't get it. He's angry.

Who does he think he is?

Who do any of us think we are?

He had his chance and blew it.

What can I say except I felt the same way.

But not now?

Not now.

Johnny goes to the barn. He comes back into the house and walks over to Keith.

Dad and I found these things of yours in the barn.

I thought they were lost.

What were you going to use them for?

Nothing. I just wanted them to have a home.

I was going to throw them out but Dad wouldn't let me.

Glad you didn't.

Me too.

Keith stands up and smiles at Johnny. First smile I've seen on his face.

Come on Johnny, show me that new machine of yours.

You were right Becky all along. That boy does have more than meets the eye, but it took falling down faith for me to see it.

The Pastor

Come as You Are
by Rev. Jim Conley

Heavenly Father, hear my prayer:

I have not come to you in prayer in such a long time. I remember when I last prayed thanksgiving and praise to You. Both my sons were still at home and I was a happy and proud man. When my son left with the funds from his share of my property I would not pray praise and thanksgiving to You because I was bitter and broken-hearted. My second son was lost and dead to me.

Now, today was the happiest day of my life. MY SON IS HOME! This son of mine was dead and is alive again; once he was lost and now he is found. When I recognized him my heart was filled with joy. I could see that he was tired and afraid and hungry. When I saw him coming I was filled with compassion and ran to throw my arms around him. I had a slave bring him my finest robe; put a ring on his finger and sandals upon his feet. I had them kill the fatted calf for a feast of celebration with music and dancing. I tell you heavenly father, it is a joy to have him back no matter what trouble he has been in and no matter what he wants from me. I praise you and thank you for all your blessings in this world. I pray that you receive me who has strayed from you for so long with the same welcome and joy. I also ask for your help and guidance at this time, dear God.

With all the joy this day has brought me, I understand Lord, that my life is suddenly far more complicated. Please lead me on the right paths for my family as I must decide so many things. This son, my prodigal son, has taken his inheritance, half my fortune, and squandered it on extravagant living. Before he left that place and returned to me he ended up working in the fields feeding swine, willing to eat what they eat. This son, my son, in his own words said to me, "Father, I have sinned against heaven and in your sight, and am no longer worthy to be called your son." My God, to look at this son whom I thought dead, to see him, to hug him has changed my life. I don't think I can ever look at him again without remembering the feeling of loss I had when he left. His actions, that caused me so much pain and grief, somehow have given me my greatest joy. My beloved wife always said that her love for him never diminished. I now understand that she was right. Everything has changed. Yet, this boy, who cannot seem to make a good decision, is home now and looking to work with me. Can I give him work fitting my son when I don't believe him ready for responsibility? What should I do with this son who once broke my heart and now has filled it with joy? Should I punish him for what he has done? He may expect me to, and his brother wants me to. Has his guilt and remorse been punishment enough? Should I give him the work of one of my slaves and treat him accordingly? Should I give him responsibilities of the son of the master? Help me find the right ways to treat this frustrating son. How do I love him, teach him, and keep him now that so much has changed?

And Father, please be with my elder son who stayed and has made me so proud. He has served me and never transgressed my commandments one time. He was so angry when I had the calf killed for his brother, he refused to come into the celebration. He is right, Dear Lord, I've never had a calf killed for him to enjoy with his friends. It is true, that the son that left and hurt me so has brought me joy. His brother that has worked so hard for me and been so loyal has never given me such joy. How do I show my loyal son how I love him and honor him? I reminded him that what is mine is his as he has always been with me, but he is still so angry. How do I show him the confidence I have in him? I know I have not shown him my love the way I should. I have expected much of him and received much from him, yet I have not taken the time to show him how proud I am of him, how much I depend on him, how much I believe in him. Help me God to show my love to this fine son of mine. I need my elder son to accept my younger son if my household is to be a household. Help me to teach my elder son forgiveness and compassion as you have taught me. I don't know who he is angrier at, his brother for squandering his part of my fortune on extravagant living or me, who welcomed his brother back with joy and love and a feast that I never gave him. Help me to help him to heal. He is mature and responsible and will be a husband and father before long. Maybe I can talk to him about fatherhood so that he may learn from the experience of having a child go astray. If my family has a future, my sons must get along and learn to work together. Please Lord; send your grace upon them.

Mostly Father, it is I who needs you. I come to you tired, afraid, and hungry for You, your love, and your grace. I have thought many times that I can be hard to live with, which might be the reason that my son left in the first place. I have not loved as you show us to love. I have not been forgiving as you teach us to forgive. I have been more harsh and less gentle than I should. I have much to be thankful for yet I have shown more pride than thanksgiving. I have not been the father that I wish to be to both my sons. Mostly I have strayed from You. I feel like my son who wandered away to waste his gifts, only to come back to me in time of need. So too, I have done this to you. Forgive me Father, for I have sinned against heaven and against you. I believe in You and ask for another chance. I am giving my prodigal son a second chance and I ask the same from you. As he needs me, I need you. I pray I will hold him to me with my love so he will never stray again. Help me, hold me, grapple me to you so I will never stray again. I need to think of what is best to do. But more importantly, I must have an open heart for both my sons and treat them as you show me. If I can love with your love, I can show them how they too can love as you want them to love.

If I reconcile with my elder son by showing him my love, he might heal and learn to love in a way that can reconcile him to his brother. If I give my younger son the right work for him, without the responsibilities that get him into trouble, yet with the opportunity to earn the respect of others, he might love himself and rid himself of his self-loathing. Our only chance is love. Love of family, each other, and God is our only chance. That starts with me, Lord, *your* prodigal son. I am truly sorry for my sins and pray that I never stray from you again.

The Critique

Both of these first-person narrative sermons are solid and provocative. Frankly, for first attempts and first drafts, these sermons are quite remarkable. Generally speaking, I was not surprised by the choices the pastor and the playwright made. The pastor chose to deal with the story in a fairly straightforward manner. Jim retold the story of the prodigal son with some creative angles but stayed fairly close to the biblical story line. The playwright took far more dramatic liberty with the text. Leslie's character's voice was wonderfully rich and real, though the point of her message was a bit more vague than one might expect from a sermon.

It was interesting that both the pastor and the playwright chose the father as the character to be dramatized. The father represents God in the parable, so it was interesting to find both the pastor and the playwright representing a rather confused and uncertain God-character. Neither father had a good handle on what do with, or what to expect from, their sons.

The choice of dramatic focus was also interesting and likely would serve as the greatest challenge to the delivery of each of these sermons. The pastor chose to address God in a prayer, and the playwright chose to have the father address his deceased wife. While there may be some textual conflict in having the God-character praying to God, the real challenge in both sermons is where the preacher would focus his attention during delivery. Typically in a sermon, you want to establish rapport with the congregation. Eye contact is the primary means of establishing that rapport. Often, it is most effective if the character you are portraying can speak directly to the congregation. Having a character praying to God, or having a graveside conversation with a deceased spouse, doesn't allow much opportunity to visually connect with the congregation.

113

The choices of setting were also quite telling. The pastor chose to represent the parable in its original context, whereas the playwright chose to place the parable in a more contemporary setting. This significant difference likely corresponds to the pastor's and playwright's views of scripture. The pastor understands that the ancient Word has something to say to us in the twenty-first century, while the more secular playwright makes the assumption that for the Bible to be relevant to us today, it has to be updated for our contemporary audience. Both choices can convey the story of the prodigal son effectively, but the choices themselves say much about the respective beliefs and understandings of scripture.

The real difference in these two sermons is the texture of the character's voice. While the story lines are virtually the same, the playwright has crafted a far richer and more engaging dramatic monologue. The father's voice in Leslie's sermon just seems more natural than the father's voice in Jim's sermon. Undoubtedly, this results from Leslie's years of study and practice of writing character. Leslie's dramatic monologue includes plenty of additional information that may not directly further the plot but does much to establish character. Take a look at any of Leslie's paragraphs, and you will see how she adds creative information that helps to paint a picture not only of a character but also of the story being told.

> Johnny and I don't talk about Keith much. We talk about you some and how we miss your laughing or teasing us, or some silly memory like when that horse threw you and you kicked it. But not Keith, till the other day when Johnny found an old box in the barn full of stuff Keith had collected—bird feathers, rocks, a chipmunk skull. We just looked at the pieces for a while. "Wonder what he was going to do with these?" That's all Johnny said. Then he closes the box up and is about to throw it away, but I stop him and I put it back on the shelf. Like that time

I found your hairbrush in the bottom of the drawer and put it back like you might come back to reclaim it. Did I think Keith would come back? Did I hope he might? I was afraid he was joining you in death and my heart was closing up to you both.

The image of Becky kicking the horse not only gives us an image of who she was, but also gives us some insight into who Keith might be, and who the father has chosen to be in relationship with. While we don't necessarily know what a chipmunk skull has to do with God welcoming us back as we are, it helps us to envision the box that Johnny has found. Again, the father's response to Becky's hairbrush sheds so much light on the father's heart and his hurt, that we can't help but have our imagination captured by the father's character. These seemingly insignificant details are exactly what natural or real dialogue and monologue contain. Leslie's use of pauses, hesitations, repeated words, and incomplete sentences further enhance our sense that the character before us is a real person. Here is a good example:

And you know Johnny, he doesn't ask for much. You know that. He has a plan, follows through, and gets the job done. Like me. But Keith.

"But Keith" is a perfect example of how to write as people actually talk. The novice dramatist, or the pastor who is writing a first-person narrative sermon, would likely finish the sentence by having the character say what does not really need to be said. *"But Keith never follows through, Keith never gets the job done."* A simple *"But Keith"* says it all. This short passage is written exactly as someone would actually speak.

In the final analysis, it is likely that Jim's sermon would communicate the central point of the biblical text more effectively, while Leslie's sermon would be more engaging for the congregation. The key is finding ways to effectively communicate the central point of a sermon, while allowing the congregation to be drawn into the story by a real, flesh-and-blood biblical character.

The Learnings

We can learn quite a bit from this experiment. There are significant challenges to delivering a first-person narrative sermon to a disembodied character (such as God) instead of relating directly to the congregation during the sermon. Always try to have your character speak directly to your congregation. We can see the value in taking some artistic and creative liberties to make a character real. At the same time, we need to realize that taking too much liberty can begin to obscure the central point of the biblical text. Feel free to get creative, but don't get so creative you free yourself from scripture. It is also evident how much more richly a character can be drawn when a pastor writes as people speak. Repeat words and phrases. Use pauses and incomplete sentences. There is no need for Kate L. Turabian to be a first-person narrative preacher's best friend!

Another Take

Finally, I want to offer you an example of what the story of the prodigal son can look like when a preacher takes plenty of artistic license while solidly maintaining the central point of the biblical text. As you read, ask yourself if this sounds like an actual person speaking. Is the Citizen Employer believable? Does he seem real? At the same time, do you come away with a clear sense of the biblical message?

The Citizen Employer

Do you remember the famine we had a few years back? I just bumped into this kid down at the market—Jewish kid. I'd nearly forgotten about him. During the last famine, when everyone was looking for work, this Jewish kid comes knocking on my door. He wanted a job.

I feel the same way you do about Jews. *Chosen people?* They think they're better than us. Won't eat our food. Won't sit at our tables. Call us dirty—*unclean*. No way was I going to hire some Jewish kid to work on my farm. *"Get the hell outta here,"* I told him.

But this kid presses me. He tells me this hard-luck story. He had his father split his inheritance between himself and his older brother, then he went to the city and blew it all. Prostitutes. Drinking. Hotels. So, I say, *"So you're not only a Jew, you're a dumb Jew. Why am I going to hire some dumb Jew to work for me?"* He said, *"Please."*

That's when it hit me. This was an opportunity. A Jew wants to work for *me*. Okay. *"I'll choose you,"* I said. I paid him next to nothing. I had no idea how he'd survive.

He showed up for his first day and I said, *"Chosen One"*—that's what we called him—*"Chosen One, shine my boots." "Chosen One, pick that up." "Chosen One—do this or that."* Hilarious. So that first day I say, *"Chosen One, I'm going to show you how special you are."* I handed him a shovel and said, *"You're going to clean out my pig pens."* You should have seen his face—a Jew knee-deep in pig slop. I said, *"Go clean out those pig pens and then come talk to me about being dirty—unclean."*

This goes on for weeks. *"Hey, Chosen One, how are those pigs?"* Some of my men told me this kid was so hungry he'd eat the pods we feed to the pigs. They wanted to know if they could give him some. No way. He's making money. He wants to eat pods, let him go out and buy some.

Last day he worked for me, I had gotten up before dawn. I went down to the pens. There's the Jewish kid, he's on his hands and knees. He's digging in the mud for the pods that had fallen to the ground that were trampled under the hooves. He was putting the pods in his mouth. I said, *"What on earth are you doing?"* He stood up. Mud running down his chin, down his chest. *"I'm hungry."* He began to cry. He said his father's hired men would never have to scrounge for food. I said, *"Then go home."* *"I can't do that. After what I did. My father would never welcome me back—my brother—never."*

I don't know why I did what I did next. But I had the Jewish kid come up to the house, had him clean up, and then I told him. *"I've got two boys myself. Young. And they're already hellions. My wife and I—when we tuck them in bed at night—we don't pray like I've seen you do, but we have this ritual. Every night we say to our boys—we do this as much for us as for them—we say to our two sons, 'If all the boys in the whole wide world were lined up in one great big huge enormous line, and your mother and I could only choose two of those boys for our sons, we would go down that line—there would be boys from Egypt, Mesopotamia, Assyria, Babylon, and from the lands in the East—and we would stop in front of you two, and we would choose you. Even when we know you—good and bad—your mother and I would still choose you to be our sons. We choose you, because we love you.'"* I told this Jewish kid that I don't know about Jews being chosen people, but I believe sons will always be chosen by their fathers. That was the last day that kid worked for me.

So, I bumped into that Jewish kid in the market the other day. He walked right up to me. The Chosen One. I didn't recognize him—the robe, the rings—he was dressed better than I was. He came up to me and simply said, *"Thank you."* He told me his father went out to the front of his property every morning since he left. He got down on his knees and prayed for his son to return. The day he left my farm, before that kid even reached his father's house, his father came running out, threw his arms around him, and kissed his neck.

It was good to see that kid again. I really didn't know what would happen if he returned home. For me, it's just further proof that there isn't a father in heaven or on earth who wouldn't choose his son all over again if he had the chance. That's worth remembering.

The Critique

This is a wonderful and brief example of a first-person narrative sermon. The descriptive nature of this sermon brings the story alive. We can hear the mocking words being spoken time and time again, "Chosen One, Chosen One." We get a fairly graphic image of the prodigal son digging pods out of the mud and eating them, with the mud running down his chin. And what is particularly engaging and unique about this sermon is that we see some character development. The Citizen Employer is transformed before our very eyes. At first, he is vindictive and cruel, but by the end he has become, if not friendly, clearly someone who possesses a compassionate heart. By the end of the sermon, the main point is clear and remains true to the biblical story: *"There isn't a father in heaven or on earth who wouldn't choose his son all over again if he had the chance."* So, come as you are.

9

Examining First-Person Narrative Sermons

The Examples

Actors make a habit of going to the theater, filmmakers go to see all the movies they can, dancers have season tickets to the ballet. As preachers we must approach our craft with a similar discipline. I believe that those of us who preach should regularly read sermons, go to hear different preachers, and even watch preachers on television. The more preaching we experience—both good preaching and bad preaching—the more adept we will become in crafting and delivering our own sermons. Realizing that there are relatively few opportunities to experience solid first-person narrative sermons, I have included a few additional sermons for your consideration and reflection.

What follows are three examples of effective first-person narrative sermons. Each one has its strengths as well as its flaws. Each sermon will be followed by a critique and suggested learnings that can be gleaned from the narrative. As you read, continue to take note of what works and what doesn't. When studying any sermon form, whether you are in worship, watching a preacher on television, or reading a sermon that is in print, always take time to examine what makes that particular message effective or ineffective. As a preacher, you should always be looking for ways to continue to learn about and hone your craft. The more sermons you read, the more sermons you hear, the more sermons you critique, the more equipped you will be to craft effective sermons yourself. That is the intent of this chapter. Read. Critique. Learn.

Hagar (Genesis 16)
by Rev. Debbie Spratley

I hate my name. One of the most important things parents are supposed to do before a child is born is to pick a name that tells the world who their child is. My parents called me Hagar, which means foreigner or wanderer. For me it was prophetic. Since Abram acquired me in Egypt many years ago I have traveled through Canaan serving his wife Sarai. During those years Sarai repeatedly told the stories of God's promises to Abram of a wealth of land and numberless descendants. At first she told them with hopeful expectation and joy, but after many years her telling became wistful and sad. No matter how hard or long she prayed, I don't think her prayers were heard, because they were never answered.

Eventually Sarai's impatience got the better of her, and she told me, "Hagar, you're going to marry Abram!" There was no discussion because, you see, the law said that if Sarai was barren, she could give me to Abram, and any child I bore would belong to Sarai and Abram.

I was pretty unhappy with the plan, but being a slave I had no choice.

As soon as it became obvious that I had conceived, Abram put me out of the marriage bed and sent me back to Sarai. I mistakenly thought she would receive me with joy and elevate my position. I was so wrong. Instead she criticized me and grumbled to others that a foreigner should not bear the child of promise. She forced me to do the heaviest chores, even sending me for water during the heat of the day. I held my tongue, but my eyes must have oozed the contempt I felt.

One day, when I was returning from the well I saw her approach Abram. And I made it my business to stop and eavesdrop. She complained to Abram about my attitude and blamed him for the events that *she* had put into place. She was even bold enough to demand that God find that the fault for the whole situation was his alone.

She demanded that Abram deal with the situation. Well, he couldn't get to the water jar fast enough to wash his hands of the whole affair. He told Sarai, "She's your slave girl. Do as you please with her." And so Sarai treated me even more harshly. Why, she even hit me. When that started I knew I had only two choices: I could flee or I could stay, but there was nothing to stay for. *I had no faith* in a God you couldn't see, and who didn't fulfill promises. *I had no hope* for my future: I would always be an abused slave. *I had no prospect of love:* my child would be taken from me and I would have no opportunity for a family of my own. I had *no faith, no hope, and no love.* . . .

And so, in the dark of night I fled toward my home village in Egypt, where I would be a foreigner and a wanderer no longer. And, as I left, I turned and I think I saw Sarai watching me go. She didn't raise an alarm; she simply turned and went back into her tent.

And I can see the question that you are dying to ask me, "If you were safely away, whatever possessed you to come back?"

I wish I had an easy answer. As I wandered in the desert two nights later I was cold and tired and hungry and thirsty. Even though I was afraid I might die, I would never go back. When I came to a small spring I fell beside it and wept.

A soft noise made me look up, and I saw a man standing by the spring. I hadn't heard or seen him approach, but for some reason I wasn't afraid. I was surprised when the stranger said my name and knew that I was Sarai's slave girl. When he asked where I was coming from and where I was going, I told him I was running away from my mistress. I didn't get to tell him my destination because he said to me, "Return to your mistress, and submit to her."

But before I could adamantly refuse to return to Sarai, he made a promise to me that sounded familiar. I would have too many offspring to count. And then more words of promise fairly poured off his tongue. I would have a son. I would call him *Ishmael:* that means *God hears*. He said that my son would be a "wild ass of a man." Now I know that that would unsettle some of you, but I somehow knew that I would never have to sacrifice my son to the hands of Abram and Sarai because asses aren't animals of sacrifice. My son would not be a slave like his mother, and he would have the skills to survive in a world of difficulty despite being assailed by his kin.

I felt a sudden chill of terror when I realized that it was the God of Abram who was making these promises to me, Hagar, a slave. If this was Abram's God, then I must surely die. But He saw my terror and gently reassured me saying, "Your pain cried out for justice. You will not suffer for the sins of Abram and Sarai." And so I named the man by the spring *El Roi*, *God of Seeing*, for he looked upon me, and I looked upon him, and I lived.

And I returned here with a heart full of the promises that would allow me to survive. I returned with *faith*. I had never believed in the God of Abram, but I know now that Abram's God is my God, El Roi.

I returned with *love* for God in my heart. With God's love and the love of my son, I know I can survive whatever befalls me.

124

And I returned with *hope,* the hope that my son's life will be better than mine.

I must admit that some of the bitterness that I felt left my heart when I told Abram that I had seen his God and had lived. And my homecoming was sweetened when I repeated the words of promise that God had offered on behalf of my son, telling him that God had taken the prerogative of naming our son *Ishmael, God Hears.*

And so, now, I perform my tasks willingly: for each time I hear someone call my son's name, which usually means he is up to some mischief, I am reminded that God does indeed see and hear our distress, and answers prayer.

I suppose that the best answer that I can give to the question "Why did I return?" is that because of my encounter with El Roi during my time of deepest despair, I discovered that within me faith, hope, and love abide, these three; and the greatest of these is . . . well . . . I really don't know which is the greatest. But what I do know is that I still hate my name. It just doesn't fit me right now, because I am not a foreigner and I am not a wanderer. I am a slave girl who is safely at home in the heart of God.

The Critique

This is an effective first-person narrative sermon. From the very first sentence, we are sucked into the drama: *"I hate my name."* Immediately, the congregation wonders why. We are at once thrown off balance and intrigued. We want to know why the preacher hates her name. When we find out a few lines later that it is the character of *Hagar* who hates her name, we are already hooked. The way the narrative is bookended is masterful. In the beginning, Hagar hates her name because she hates that she is a wanderer and a foreigner. She hates being a slave. She hates that she has no faith, no hope, and no love. By the end of the narrative, after her encounter with God, she still hates her name, but for a different reason. Hagar's name no longer accurately describes who she is. She now has faith, she has hope, she has love, and she has found a home in the heart of God.

The only thing this sermon lacks is the creative touches a seasoned dramatist would include. We don't have a clear picture of her setting. We could use a better description of Abram and Sarai by the well. What did they look like? What were their facial expressions? Did they whisper, did they shout, were they conscious of those around them as they argued? What did El Roi look like? Describe the spring by which the encounter took place. Did any of Hagar's experiences remind her of past memories? If so, take time to describe them. There could have been much more description in this sermon.

And, finally, as wonderful as this first-person narrative is, there is no way Hagar the slave girl would speak as cleanly as she does. The image we get of Hagar is that of a polished orator who has a perfectly edited narrative to share with her audience. This sermon is very good, and if the preacher were to rough it up around the edges a bit, it would be even better.

The Learnings

Don't be afraid to present the biblical narrative in its actual time and setting. Trust in the power that can be experienced when you take your congregation back into the biblical world, and resist the temptation to make the biblical world step into the twenty-first century. Try to hook your audience early on. The more you keep them guessing, the more likely they are to stay with you. Just remember to tie it all together by the end of your sermon. Take some detours. Chase some rabbits down their holes.

Allow your congregation to meander around antiquity with you for a while. Paint a picture. Describe where you are, what you are seeing, and how you are feeling. And finally, take some rough-grain sandpaper and run it over the sermon. Rough things up a bit. And don't hesitate to run some of your grammar through the shredder.

Joshua (Deuteronomy 34:1–12)
by Rev. Eric Dupee

Moses is dead! We knew it would happen sooner than later, but you're never quite prepared to lose someone like him. Recently he said to me, "Joshua, I need you. Your people need you. I don't know how much longer I have, but with me or without me, this people must take possession of the land that God promised."

So, Moses assigned me the task of leading you across the Jordan River. And frankly, I'm as nervous as you are. God was clearly with Moses. You remember what it was like to be around him. You never knew what to expect. One moment we were cursing him for leading us into the desert. We were cornered, with Egyptian soldiers breathing down our necks. The next moment, Moses stretched out his hand, and the sea opened up before us. Or how about when he climbed Mt. Sinai to receive the Ten Commandments the second time, for reasons I won't mention. Do you remember how his face shined upon his return?

I'm no babe in the woods, but I've been asking the same questions you are. Without Moses, how will we know what to do once we cross the river? Without Moses, where will we find the courage to face the challenges that lie ahead? Without Moses, how can we be assured that God will continue to act on our behalf?

Well, before we go even one step further, there is something I want to share with you. You see, the other night when the elders were together, Moses was there. There was a discussion about who would lead in the event that Moses was no longer able. The conversation went late into the evening.

127

I just remember how cold it was. Being among the youngest present, I got up from my seat to tend the fire. After adding a log, I gazed at the flames for just a moment, taking in the warmth. When I noticed Moses walking in my direction, I assumed he was getting up in order to speak to someone behind me. But when he came next to me he stopped, placed his hands on my shoulders, and in sight of everyone said, "It is Joshua who will lead my people. I give him my blessing."

I was blessed by Moses!

I always assumed that my day would come, but Moses said it would be me and it would be now. I recalled all the times over the years that he had taken me into his confidence. I remembered all I learned by watching the way he interacted with people. I remembered his infectious passion for the Lord and for each of you. I've been prepared to lead for some time, but for some reason I needed to hear those words.

Have you ever had someone you revere tell you you're blessed? It's the most amazing feeling. Suddenly, you begin to see yourself in a whole new way. You may not have had this experience, but when somebody tells you you're blessed, you begin to really believe you are blessed. You begin to think, "Maybe I really am capable. Maybe I really am destined for something more."

And placing his hands on me just anchored that feeling. He made a physical connection with me, but it was so much more than that. I felt his power and his passion and his energy fill my being. It was like when you light one candle with the flame of another. He maintained his own light, yet he passed it on to me. But the most important thing was that he placed his trust in me. Moses trusted me.

Even though he said I would lead, I never dreamed I could fill his shoes. I still don't, but he laid his hands on me and blessed me, and that was what I needed to step up to the task. I have this new sense of courage. I have greater expectations. I have a new-found confidence that we will be successful in the task before us.

Moses assigned me to lead you, and here's what I want you to do. I want you to call your children together and gather whatever family you have. Then, begin pulling up your tent stakes and packing up your belongings. It's time to leave this place and enter into our new life on the other side of the Jordan. That's our destiny.

But before you cross that river, I want you to do something. I want you to find someone to bless. I want you to empower someone the way you were empowered. There is someone in your life, maybe even in this room, that needs to hear an encouraging word. There is someone who looks up to you, who reveres you. It may be your son or your daughter. It may be a neighbor or a friend. This person has the skills and maturity to take on a great task, and all he or she needs is your blessing.

Before dying, Moses offered the words that would set me free to accomplish my task. Don't wait until it's too late. Don't die without blessing someone. There is someone who needs to hear the words that you have to say. And so, today, who will you set free?

The Critique

This is another fine example of first-person narrative preaching. We are not only placed directly in the biblical world, but are given our own role to play. We are the Israelites, and Joshua is preparing to give us a task. The description of the blessing at the fire is wonderfully textured. As a listener or a reader, we can almost feel the warmth of the moment and the flames. *Being among the youngest present, I got up from my seat to tend the fire. After adding a log, I gazed at the flames for just a moment, taking in the warmth. When I noticed Moses walking in my direction, I assumed he was getting up in order to speak to someone behind me . . . he stopped, placed his hands on my shoulders, and in sight of everyone said, "It is Joshua who will lead my people. I give him my blessing." Tossing a log on the fire,*

129

staring at the fire, taking in the warmth of the fire are not necessary to tell the story, but they are essential ingredients that help to bring the story alive. And again, the preacher creatively illustrates for us the feeling of being blessed: *I felt his power and his passion and his energy fill my being. It was like when you light one candle with the flame of another. He maintained his own light, yet he passed it on to me.* That is dramatic monologue at its best—taking an idea and turning it into an image that sticks in our minds and warms our hearts. And by the end of this sermon, we are ready to offer that same kind of blessing to someone in our own lives. This is a brief, concise, creative, and deeply moving first-person narrative sermon.

The Learnings

You don't have to go long to go deep! Don't be afraid of brevity. Offering your people a snapshot of a biblical character can be far more effective than trying to give them a feature-length film.

As frequently as you are able, take your characters' ideas and turn them into images. Ideas can be forgotten, images can be unforgettable. I may not understand blessing, but I have lit enough candles to know what Joshua is describing.

Don't shy away from giving your parishioners a character or a role to play. The ultimate goal of preaching is to get our people to live the text. What better way for people to take up residence in scripture than to give them a name and an address!

The Scribe (Mark 12:28–34)
by Rev. Stephen Chapin Garner

I am here because of my parents. They were not wealthy people, but they saved enough to place me in a

130

school that taught me to read and write. *"That's the key,"* my father would say, *"that's the key to getting ahead in this life—you've got to know something up here. Education is the key—the key,"* he would say, and pound the table. You see, my father worked with his hands all his life as a stone mason, and he knew that those who accumulated wealth and stature were people who worked with their heads. My parents wanted me to have opportunities they did not. So they saved and sacrificed. I understood the sacrifices they made for me, and so I have worked as hard as I can in hopes of making them proud. I was not the first or the brightest in my class, but I made sure no one worked harder than me. So here I am. A scribe in the temple. I make good money, and I work in the most sacred institution in our land. I have a loving wife and two wonderful children. My parents died a few years ago. First my father, and then my mother the following year. To this day I work hard so that if they are looking down upon me they can be proud—they can know that the sacrifices they made for me were worthwhile.

Now, I love my father, he was the man I wanted to grow up to be. I only hope I am half the father and husband he was. However, I now doubt both his *key to life,* and the worth of the sacrifices he and my mother made for me . . . thus, I fear they are not proud . . . and that breaks my heart.

My job as a scribe in the temple is simple. I am never to be heard, and I am only to be seen when called for by one of the Pharisees or another member of the Sanhedrin Council. Scribes can do many things—record the proceedings of the council, draft notes and other correspondence for temple authorities, some of us transcribe the Torah and other sacred text so that they can be read in the assembly and elsewhere. *I* am specifically responsible for transcribing our code of laws. I sit in a small room and copy the Mosaic law, the Levitical law, and the Rabbinical law. I am responsible for copying all of them, nearly nine hundred different laws (depending on how you count them). I know them all by heart.

Command #33 instructs me on how I am to press and care for these robes. Command #224 lets us know how many lashes to give a person who breaks a law. Command #360 instructs a person on how to sever the head of a bird when making a sin offering. I know them all. I am able to write the entire code out three times in a day on papyrus scrolls. Some scribes' scrolls are done with more artistry than mine, but no one produces as many scrolls as I do.

I've been a scribe for nearly sixteen years now, I've lost count of how many scrolls I have produced. I confess I am weary. I am numb. The law. The rules. The commandments. They have become a blur. They have become words on a page for me. Words on a page— nothing more. I have seen people beaten and whipped because of these words. I have seen people stoned to death because of these words. I have seen friendships broken apart because of these words. Fists have been thrown in this very temple because of these words . . . words I write out three times a day, every day—except on the Sabbath. So many times I have wanted to speak up—to speak out—but scribes are not to be heard from or seen unless requested. And being a good scribe—trying to be the best scribe—is the way I honor my parents.

A prophet came to Jerusalem a few days ago. The religious leaders don't call him a prophet, but the people do. He came in on a donkey, and we heard that the people laid their coats—their cloaks—down on the ground so that he might ride over them. The people even tore branches off the trees and waved them in the air, shouting and cheering. They were calling him Messiah. He made a beeline for the temple, and he has been teaching the people here in the temple for the last couple of days.

The Pharisees, most of the scribes, and the entire council are beside themselves with anger. *"How dare this Nazarene, this son of a carpenter, come into our temple and teach our people?"* They would have immediately thrown him out on his head, if it had not been for the crowds. The crowds that gather to hear him teach are enormous.

I can hardly get through them in the morning to get to my work. I had heard this prophet's name before, but even when he was teaching I couldn't pay much attention to him. The Pharisees and the other scribes were having secret meetings about him, but I didn't attend. I had work to do.

But yesterday, all the temple leaders confronted this man called Jesus. I had known beforehand what they had planned to do. They were going to attempt to turn the crowd against him, and they planned to trick him into denouncing the emperor. One way or another, this Nazarene carpenter was going to be removed from the temple.

So yesterday, I put my scrolls down, and I went to hear and see what was going to happen. I pressed my way into the temple assembly. The other scribes were surprised to see me, I think.

I have never witnessed the assembly so full and so quiet. People were spellbound. The voice of this man teaching was both confident and compassionate. He spoke with the authority—as one who knew both the scriptures and the presence of God. Without even hearing his teaching—his presence was . . . he just is one of those people you know is holy. No wonder the Pharisees were nervous. He was speaking the truth about God in simple ways, in ways that people could really understand—even the children understood. *"How should I explain the love of God to you?"* he said. *"How many of you having a hundred sheep, upon losing one of them, does not go out leaving the ninety-nine behind to go after the lost one? And when found, which of you does not lay the lamb on your shoulders carrying it home. That is how much God loves you, to seek you out at all cost when you are lost."* He told stories. He smiled. When he spoke it was as if he was speaking directly to you.

But then, the chief priest directed a group of Pharisees to question Jesus. One of them called out from the crowd, *"Teacher, we know that you are sincere and teach the truth about God. Tell us, should we pay taxes to the Caesar, or*

should all our offerings be made to God alone?" I knew
what they were doing. They were setting this Nazarene
up. It was a brilliant question—brilliant, and evil. Jesus
was either going to have to claim that all offerings must
go to God, thus provoking the wrath of the Romans, or
he would have to endorse taxes and thus endorse the
emperor as a god. There was no way out for him.

Jesus paused for a moment, and then he said, *"You are
testing me. Give me a denarius."* One of the scribes tossed
him a coin. Then, looking at the coin, Jesus asked, *"Whose
face is this, and whose title is on this coin?"* The Pharisee
asking the question replied, *"The Emperor's."* Jesus tossed
the coin back and said, *"Give to the Emperor the things
that are his, and offer to God that which is God's."* I was
stunned. A perfectly faithful answer. You should have
seen the look on the chief priest's face. The chief priest
was being outdone in his own temple!

And then another Pharisee asked a question about
resurrection and about the Mosaic law. It was an absurd
question about a man having seven brothers, marrying
the same woman, and being faithful to the Torah.

Now, I know the law—the *entire* law, and the Pharisees were twisting the law in an attempt to discredit this
man—what they were doing, in my opinion, was offensive,
and the people knew it. But with every single question,
Jesus responded with answers that both confounded and
embarrassed the priests and made them silent.

After a moment or two, a final voice broke the silence.
The voice trembled and cracked. It was a voice that had
never been heard in the temple before. It was a voice
almost unfamiliar to me—it was *my* voice. I do not know
what had gotten into me, but I asked a question. I hadn't
been planning on asking anything. Speaking in the holy
places is not my role. But my voice, quivering and uncertain, became audible. It was as if I was watching myself
speak, and I was astounded at myself—the audacity . . .
but I wanted to know—I had to know. Of all the hundreds of laws I have written down, of all the thousands
of times I had written them . . . I asked, *"Teacher, which*

134

commandment is first of all?" Every member of the Sanhedrin Council stared me down . . . but for some reason,
I just had to know. I was scared, had I just lost my job?
But then *he* looked at me and smiled. I think Jesus could
tell I wasn't trying to trick him.

This man from Nazareth, a carpenter's son—just like I
am a stone mason's son—he looked at me and said, "It is
not so complicated as you make it. You need know only
two commands. *The first is, 'The Lord is one, you shall love
the Lord your God with all your heart, with all your soul,
with all your mind, and with all your strength.' And the
second is this, 'You shall love your neighbor as yourself.'
There is no commandment greater than these."* He looked
even more intently at me and said, "That is all you ever
need to write. That is all you ever need to know."

I could not speak. There was no breath in my chest.
He had taken the nearly nine hundred laws I knew by
heart, and summed them up in two simple commands.
Suddenly, and seemingly for the first time, my faith made
sense . . . my faith seemed manageable—possible. Love
God, love one another. Anyone could understand that.
Anyone could do that.

No one dared ask Jesus any other questions. For my
part, I sat down and listened to his teaching throughout
the night.

I do not know if this Jesus from Nazareth is a prophet,
I do not know if he is Messiah, or Lord, or Savior. All I
know is that I can no longer live my life as I have. I cannot be a temple scribe. I cannot copy down law day and
night. Life is not about law, it is about love. Loving God.
Loving neighbor. Loving friend and foe alike.

It is that simple, and I cannot go back. Will my parents
be proud? Perhaps not. But I have realized, the real key to
life is not what you know, but what you do, and how you
love. That is what I will teach my children. Of course, I met
this prophet because I worked in the temple, I worked in
the temple because I could read and write, and I could read
and write because my parents put me through school. Perhaps they will find some pride in that after all. AMEN.

The Critique

I leave this final critique for you, the reader. This was the very first first-person narrative sermon I ever delivered. It demonstrates both the promise and the weakness of any preacher who is trying to stretch and develop himself or herself into a skilled artisan and craftsman. Take time to go back over the text of "The Scribe," and see for yourself if I was then practicing what I am now preaching. Be exacting in your critique. Did I captivate the reader's attention from the very beginning? Did I maintain dramatic tension throughout the sermon? Is the text written as people actually speak? Are ideas translated into images? Did I paint a visual image of both The Scribe's surroundings and his feelings? Was it truly a dramatic monologue? Were there obstacles to overcome? Was there a beginning, a middle, and an end? Can you remember the climax and the denouement? Was it a sermon? Was a clear biblical point conveyed? Hopefully, you are now able to readily critique a first-person narrative sermon, so that you can continue to develop your own proficiency and skill in this unique and powerful sermon style.

The Learnings

If you are able to learn anything from this sermon, I hope it is that you have to start somewhere, and you have to be willing to take risks if you want to grow. Your first sermons in this style of preaching don't have to be perfect, but if you work hard, and if you are diligent about studying the craft of dramatic monologue, you will find a new and effective avenue to stretch and grow your congregation's faith.

10

Resources for Further Study of Dramatic Monologue

How Do I Continue to Learn?

There is simply no reason for the creation and delivery of weak or misdirected first-person narrative sermons when there is such an enormous collection of dramatic resources and dramatic monologues for pastors to tap into and study. In almost every major city in our country that has a thriving theatrical community, you will find bookshops dedicated to the dramatic arts. Wander into any of these establishments, and you will be taken aback by the countless volumes on display that feature collections of dramatic monologues, as well as books that can aid people in the delivery of those monologues. The dramatic talent, namely actors, upon whom our country's multibillion-dollar entertainment industry is built, are constantly in search of new, fresh, and undiscovered monologues. Every actor needs to have at least two classical and two contemporary audition monologues prepared at all times. Almost all initial dramatic auditions require an actor to deliver one or more of their monologues. This is an absolute boon for pastors who are interested in developing their abilities to craft and deliver first-person narrative sermons. There are literally millions of monologues out there for us to read, study, critique, and learn from. Monologue collections are filled with quality monologues from films, television shows, and plays. There are even books that are designed to help actors write their own monologues. Simply picking up one or two of these volumes, and reading a brief dramatic monologue from time to time, can greatly enhance your understanding of how effective dramatic monologues work. I cannot stress enough how easily dramatic monologues are obtained, and how helpful they are to our craft. It amazes me that as preachers of first-person narrative sermons, we have not yet discovered this ocean of resources. I have no doubt that the number of volumes on preaching published each year would be dwarfed by the resources produced to help actors find, prepare, create, and deliver dynamic and captivating dramatic monologues. Remember, a first-person narrative sermon is simply a dramatic monologue that conveys a biblical principle or idea.

The Resources

So, just how does a pastor get a hold of these resources? The Internet is the easiest place to start, but I would be remiss if I didn't share with you what is probably the most enjoyable and creatively inspiring place to start. If you are ever in New York City, you must visit the Drama Book Shop at 250 West 40th Street. The Drama

Book Shop is a New York institution. It is filled from floor to ceiling with resources for anyone who has the slightest interest in the dramatic arts. The Drama Book Shop staff are gracious, impassioned, and exhaustively knowledgeable about drama. You can simply squeeze your way through the constant stream of actors milling around the bookshelves, find a staff person, tell them what a first-person narrative sermon is, let them know you are looking for resources on the development and delivery of dramatic monologues, and they will direct you to the resources that will be most helpful to you. You will need to ask for assistance, not because these resources are difficult to find, but rather, because there are so many resources at The Drama Book Shop, you will need help narrowing your options. Plus, The Drama Book Shop staff will be knowledgeable about the most recent additions to their dramatic monologue collections. New volumes come out daily. Again, if you are visiting New York City, a trip to the Drama Book Shop should not be missed. You will find it to be a surprisingly entertaining experience, and you never know what theater, film, or television personality you will bump into!

Now, I know not everyone can get to Broadway to get dramatic monologue resources. The good news is that there are so many other avenues to these materials that you won't even need to leave your home to access them. You can go directly to the Internet and find everything and anything you could possibly need. Check out www. actorpoint.com, www.shakespeare-monologues.org, and www.theatrehistory.com. You can also surf sites such as www.thedramabookshop.com or those of some of the premier play-publishing companies, like www.samuel french.com and www.bakersplays.com. Even www.ama zon.com has hundreds of resources that are helpful. Go to any of these sites and simply type "monologue" in the search box, then begin sifting through the hundreds of dramatic monologue resources there. One book you should not be without is Glen Alterman's book, *Creating Your Own Monologue*. This book is a step-by-step tutorial on how to craft an effective and engaging monologue. You will likely want to look for annual collections of monologues by reputable publishers; a few of these are *The Best Stage Monologues*, published by Smith and Kraus, *Outstanding Men's Monologues* and *Outstanding Women's Monologues*, published by Dramatists Play Service, *American Theater Book of Monologues for Women* and *Contemporary American Monologues for Men*, published by Theater Communications Group. Penguin Books also has a number of helpful resources, like *The Actor's Book of Contemporary Stage Monologues: More than 150 Monologues from over 70 Playwrights*. When it comes to resources on the delivery and performance of monologues, the *Two Minutes to Shine* volumes by Samuel French are quite helpful. Sometimes, you may even find a seemingly outlandish resource that can be keenly insightful, such as *Killer Monologues: Highly Actable Monologues and Performance Tips to Give You an Almost Unfair Advantage in the Auditioning Game*, published by Impact Films. As you begin to learn about the development and delivery of first-person narrative sermons by studying dramatic monologues, you will find that just about any resource you happen upon will supply you with some nugget of unexpectedly helpful information.

The Leisurely Art of Studying Dramatic Monologue

"Writers write" is a familiar and wise mantra uttered by just about every successful creative writer in the world. Writers also read. You can't be a writer if you are not actively studying or practicing your craft. When I was acting in college, and later in New York City, my instructors and directors always told me, "You need to be going to the theater all the time. You need to know drama." You have to go and watch good acting." For whatever reason, I was never drawn to be a truly devoted student of acting. Not surprisingly, my call has not been to the stage. Interestingly, as a preacher, I have become a sermon junkie. I read every sermon I can get my hands on, I watch as many sermons as I can on television, I listen to sermons on the Internet, and I will go to hear great preaching when I am able. I find that I eagerly devour bad sermons and good sermons alike, because it is as important to know what *not* to do as it is to know what to do. I constantly want to study and learn the art of sermon development and delivery, so that I can continue to grow in my effectiveness as a preacher. Preachers preach, and preachers study sermons, as well as other preachers. When it comes to studying dramatic monologues that inform our first-person narrative sermons, the process can be as easy as it is leisurely and enjoyable. Dramatic monologue and dialogue are everywhere. You will find dramatic monologues in theatrical productions, in films, and in television programs. You will even discover dramatic monologue and dialogue in the novels and books you read. Just listen to radio programs like Garrison Keillor's *Prairie Home Companion*, and you will discover dramatic monologue at its finest. When you turn on the television, when you go to a movie, when you go to the theater, take time to really notice what the actors are doing. Notice how the actors are always "in character." When you see Meryl Streep, Dustin Hoffman, Charlize Theron, or Kenneth Branagh in a new production, even though you have seen them countless times before, they appear entirely different in their new role. They have ceased to exist as their own person and have become

141

totally immersed in their new character. Listen to the way the actors speak. Take notice of how the dialogue and monologues have been crafted. Ask the questions we have been working with in this book. What works? What doesn't? Is a particular character believable? Why? Why not? While the use of the Internet has made sermons more accessible, finding dramatic monologues is even easier. With a few keystrokes, you can find them, study them, and learn from them. It is likely you will never find studying for anything, even the art of preaching, so convenient, leisurely, and enjoyable. So, have fun studying the art of creating dramatic monologues. And then get into character!